Chiang Ching-kuo's Leadership in the Development of the Republic of China on Taiwan

Edited by
Shao-chuan Leng

Volume III
The Miller Center Series on Asian Political Leadership

UNIVERSITY
PRESS OF
AMERICA

Lanham • New York • London

The Miller Center

University of Virginia

Copyright © 1993 by
University Press of America®, Inc.
4720 Boston Way
Lanham, Maryland 20706

3 Henrietta Street
London WC2E 8LU England

All rights reserved
Printed in the United States of America
British Cataloging in Publication Information Available

Co-published by arrangement with
The Miller Center of Public Affairs,
University of Virginia

The views expressed by the author(s) of this publication do not necessarily represent the opinions of the Miller Center. We hold to Jefferson's dictum that: "Truth is the proper and sufficient antagonist to error, and has nothing to fear from the conflict, unless by human interposition, disarmed of her natural weapons, free argument and debate."

Library of Congress Cataloging-in-Publication Data

Chiang Ching-kuo's leadership in the development of the Republic of China on Taiwan / edited by Shao-chuan Leng.
  p. cm. — (The Miller Center series on Asian political leadership ; v. 3)
  Includes index.
  1. Chiang, Ching-kuo, 1910–1988. 2. Taiwan—Politics and government—1975–1988. I. Leng, Shao Chuan, 1921–   .
  II. Series.
      DS799.82.C437C4376   1992
      951.24'905—dc20   92-31103 CIP

ISBN 0-8191-8903-0 (cloth : alk. paper)
ISBN 0-8191-8904-9 (pbk. : alk. paper)

 The paper used in this publication meets the minimum requirements of American National Standard for Information Sciences—Permanence of Paper for Printed Library Materials, ANSI Z39.48–1984.

Dedicated to

Nora and David

Table of Contents

PREFACE vii
    Kenneth W. Thompson

INTRODUCTION ix
    Shao-chuan Leng

1. **HISTORICAL SETTING FOR THE RISE OF CHIANG CHING-KUO** 1
    Cho-yun Hsu

2. **CHIANG CHING-KUO'S DECISION FOR POLITICAL REFORM** 31
    Andrew J. Nathan and Helena V. S. Ho

3. **THE TAIWAN ECONOMY IN THE SEVENTIES** . . . 63
    John Fei

4. **COMMENTS ON JOHN C. FEI'S "THE TAIWAN ECONOMY IN THE SEVENTIES"** 89
    Thomas A. Metzger

5. **CCK AND SOCIETY: INSTITUTIONAL LEADERSHIP AND SOCIAL DEVELOPMENT ON TAIWAN** 103
    Edwin Winckler

6. **CHIANG CHING-KUO'S POLICIES TOWARD MAINLAND CHINA AND THE OUTSIDE WORLD** 133
    Ralph N. Clough

TABLE OF CONTENTS

7. **THE LEGACY OF CHIANG CHING-KUO: EXTERNAL ASSESSMENTS REASSESSED** 163
    Brian Hook

8. **REFLECTIONS ON LEADERSHIP, CHINA, AND CHIANG CHING-KUO** 191
    Robert A. Scalapino

EDITOR AND CONTRIBUTOR INFORMATION 209

INDEX 211

Preface

KENNETH W. THOMPSON
Director, the Miller Center of Public Affairs

The Miller Center of Public Affairs at the University of Virginia is proud of its inquiries on Asian political leadership conducted under the direction of Professor S. C. Leng. The main focus of the Miller Center has been on the study of the American presidency. Professor Leng has enabled the Center to expand its approach by introducing a new dimension of comparative studies. Two volumes have been published, one of which has been cited as among the most outstanding studies of 1990.

Professor Shmuel N. Eisenstadt has observed that "there is a large body of research that can be called 'comparative' and that it is capable of providing analytical tools of great importance. Within the limits set by methodological considerations it can contribute the framework of a common approach . . . to the understanding of the variability of major types of social phenomena." In the long run research on other political systems can contribute to a broader view of the American political system. There are lessons to be derived from a study of political leadership in Asia that have implications for understanding political leadership in the United States. New concepts and insights may result from a better understanding of Chiang Ching-kuo's leadership in the development of the Republic of China on Taiwan.

Because theories in the social science are dependent on historical information, the beginning of wisdom even for those with theoretical objectives is the study of the past. Thus, the present volume begins with a discussion of the historical setting and goes on to investigate political reform, the economy, and external relations.

The great strength of a study such as the present inquiry stems from the authoritative knowledge of authors of the individual

PREFACE

chapters. For the first time, some of the best minds in Chinese and Taiwan studies have come together to examine all aspects of Chiang Ching-kuo's legacy. It would be difficult to discover any fundamental aspect of Taiwanese society that is overlooked.

For this we can thank Professor Leng, who in a quiet but determined manner brought to fruition an idea that required patient and intelligent analysis. For those of us who have known and worked with Professor Leng, no other outcome would be conceivable. We are delighted that Leng will be continuing his leadership of Asian studies at the University of Virginia for years to come.

Introduction

SHAO-CHUAN LENG

In the 1970s and 1980s the Republic of China on Taiwan was under the direction of Chiang Ching-kuo (CCK), who served first as its Premier (1972-1978) and later as its President (1978-1988). It was during those years that Washington normalized its relations with Beijing and downgraded its ties with Taipei to an unofficial level. In the same period, however, Taiwan experienced a great developmental breakthrough and achieved what has been generally referred to as an "economic miracle." In the last few years before his death in January 1988, Chiang also took important steps to move Taiwan in the direction of democratization, e.g., permitting an opposition political party, the new Democratic Progressive party (DDP), to participate in elections in late 1986 and lifting the decree of martial law in 1987.

To evaluate Chiang Ching-kuo's leadership role in the development of the Republic of China on Taiwan, a special conference was held at the University of Virginia in March 1990 under the sponsorship of the Miller Center of Public Affairs. Revised versions of the papers presented at the conference constitute the chapters of the present volume.

Chapter One provides the historical setting. Dividing CCK's life (1910-1988) into six stages, Professor Cho-yun Hsu proceeds to discuss historical events and circumstances that were relevant to the rise of Chiang as a political leader. Among those examined are CCK's 11 years of hardship experience in Soviet Russia, political internship in Kiangsi during the war against Japan, service in the military commissar system, in intelligence and in the youth corps after moving to Taiwan, and eventual rise from the posts of defense minister and premier to the presidency of the Republic of China (ROC).

According to Hsu, CCK was brought up in an atmosphere of highly charged patriotism and Confucian-style devotion to duty. His childhood experience and socialist education in Russia also combined to influence his orientation toward populism. All this appeared to prepare Chiang well to "steer Taiwan through the difficult, choppy waters" of diplomatic setbacks and domestic agitations. In Hsu's view, it was CCK's populism, political commitment and savvy, and ability to recruit first-rate technocrats that contributed to his success in creating the economic miracle on Taiwan and moving the ROC toward fuller democratization.

In Chapter Two, Professor Andrew Nathan and Ms. Helena Ho seek to analyze Chiang Ching-kuo's motives for launching the reform in March 1986, which marked "a shift from gradual liberalization under a regime of 'soft authoritarianism' to the beginning of what seems to be a process of democratic transition." They first look at two external factors: international pressure and the PRC's threat. Then they scrutinize two factors within Taiwan: pressure from the opposition and need for reinvigoration of the KMT. Finally, two factors pertaining to Chiang himself—health and succession, political values and sense of mission—are analyzed. In each case, the authors examine how the factor in question may have appeared to Chiang and may have influenced his decision.

Nathan and Ho not only provide a clear picture of CCK's motives and style as a political leader, but they also contribute to the recent literature on transitions to democracy. Many of the findings in this chapter on Taiwan's experience, like Spain's in the 1970s, fit into Alfred Stepan's "Path 4a" ("redemocratization initiated by the civilian or civilianized political leadership"). On the other hand, as pointed out by the authors, Taiwan's case differs from that of Spain in several ways, including the existence of the China mainland factor, the starting of the transition by the leader of the old regime, and the posing of a much less serious potential challenge to the reform by the military.

There are two chapters on Taiwan's economic development under the leadership of Chiang Ching-kuo. In Chapter Three, Professor John Fei discusses the Taiwan economy with a focus on

INTRODUCTION

the 1970s. According to him, the Seventies were an important period of Taiwan's preparation for a full transition from a partially liberated economy toward liberalization and internationalization in the Eighties. In the context of the global economic slowdown, it "took a statesman with both courage and wisdom to adopt a policy of stability that was *farsighted* but *unpopular* under the milieu of the political economic culture of the Seventies."

While stressing the superiority of China's human resources because of its cultural heritage, Fei attributes Taiwan's economic success essentially to the free market system and nongovernmental intervention. The miracle would not have been possible, he argues, had CCK not had the intuitive insight to see through the evil of inflationary finance via convenience of money printing and had he not insisted on an "economic cabinet" staffed by enlightened administrators dedicated to a philosophy of monetary conservatism.

Chapter Four contains a lengthy and thoughtful commentary on Fei's paper by Professor Thomas Metzger. The author begins by praising Fei's "illuminating" work and significant conceptualization on the nature of the state's impact on the economy in the ROC. Then he raises the issue of the causes of Taiwan's economic success. From his perspective, that economic miracle cannot be explained by the market system alone; a variety of other factors must be taken into account, namely, land reform, state investments in education and in the infrastructure, state efforts to slow population growth, the relatively small size of Taiwan, the cultural inheritance, and so on.

In regard to the question of state intervention, Metzger would distinguish between undesirable intervention (such as building up a large state sector and adopting inflationary policies) and desirable intervention (such as land reform, investments in infrastructure, investments in human capital, and ecological policies). Dr. Sun Yat-sen's approach is presented as precisely emphasizing both respect for the marketplace and constructive state intervention. According to Metzger, Sun's views are actually those that have been central to ROC's economic policy since 1950, and they are neither "outdated" nor necessarily "refuted" by Fei's critique.

Chapter Five presents an evaluation of social development of Taiwan during the administration of Chiang Ching-kuo. The

INTRODUCTION

author, Professor Edwin Winckler, begins with a conceptualization of Taiwan's development from three approaches: liberal, radical, and conservative. He places the ROC's overall social policy under CCK on the conservative side with some liberal and radical elements. The second section of the chapter describes the political background of social policy on Taiwan: leadership as institution, leadership over institutions, and leadership through institutions. In the final section, Winckler surveys three levels of ROC social policy—supranational, national, and subnational—identifying programs in which CCK was involved. Supranational policies are concerned with the external and ethnic relations of Taiwan. National policies pertain to demographic (public health, population, and medicare), stratificational (class, occupation, and education), and spatial (regional planning, urban planning, and housing construction) domains.

The chapter does not claim to provide in detail the precise role of CCK in ROC social policy, but it does identify some of the intersections between Chiang's career and relevant social processes. Among the findings, CCK is said to have displayed a consistent concern for socializing youth and aiding the disadvantaged. He is also credited for allowing gradual formulation of social policies and an increasing priority for them on Taiwan's political agenda. Moreover, Chiang "helped unleash the political democratization that made such policies inevitable, and identified himself with humanist and populist values that would support them."

In Chapter Six, Professor Ralph Clough analyzes Chiang Ching-kuo's policies toward mainland China and the outside world. The period of CCK's rule is divided into two phases, 1972-78, before the United States formally recognized the PRC, and 1979-88, after the United States had severed diplomatic relations with the ROC. In Phase 1, Chiang was confronted with Washington's move toward normalizing ties with Beijing on the one hand and the PRC's combination of threats, conciliatory gestures, and efforts to isolate the ROC on the other. According to Clough, Chiang met his challenges quite well. The ROC under his guidance did its best to retain as strong a relationship as possible with the United States, especially in economic areas, while it stood firm against PRC pressures and inducements by strengthening Taiwan's economy and defenses and intensifying its substantive relations with foreign countries even without official ties.

During Phase 2, CCK continued his efforts to maintain close but "unofficial" ties with the United States within the framework of the Taiwan Relations Act (TRA). Under increasing domestic pressure, he also began to allow indirect interchange between Taiwan and mainland China. As observed by Clough, Chiang's basic goal of reunifying China under a non-Communist system remained unchanged, but he showed tactical flexibility in adjusting his policy to reality. Although differing from some of his "liberal" aides in regard to the prospects for negotiating with Beijing, he did legalize indirect travel, trade, and investment. In fact, he could portray these activities as "conveying to the people of the mainland the Taiwan experience and thus furthering progress toward the long-term goal of unifying China under a non-Communist system."

There is a Chinese saying that "only when a person is dead can he be finally judged and assessed (*gaiguan lunding*)." In Chapter Seven, Professor Brian Hook tries to evaluate CCK's legacy through the reexamination of a selection of the external assessments of Chiang's life made at the time of his death in the light of continuities in Taiwan and of events throughout the world in the final days of the 1980s. Among the assessments and eulogies were those from the PRC (at both political and personal levels), Hong Kong (*Ming Pao* and *Far Eastern Economic Review*), and Japan (*Yomiuri Shimbun* and *Asahi Shimbun*). In the United States, the *New York Times* offered an extensive coverage of CCK. For European views, the author has selected British, French, German, Swiss, and Spanish sources.

The external assessments were generally positive and gave Chiang credit for Taiwan's economic prosperity and transition toward democracy. In Hook's opinion, they were on the whole fair and accurate. Looking back over the evidence, he says, "one strand running throughout is of a successful reformer who had the necessary combination of status, experience, charisma, humanity . . . to convince conservative members of the case for reform." A significant adjustment to be made in the assessments of CCP is to recognize the "relative durability of his reform" that may prepare

INTRODUCTION

Taiwan to have a new relationship with the mainland and to play a major role in the modernization of China.

Chapter Eight, written by Professor Robert Scalapino, concludes this volume with reflections on leadership, China, and Chiang Ching-kuo. It begins by defining leadership as the capacity to influence, shape, or control decisions and actions affecting others. Among a variety of capacities for successful leadership, the author lists the ability to select the proper timing for action and the capacity and willingness to make change as dictated by circumstances. Scalapino then goes on to show the important role of leadership not only in authoritarian polities but also in democratic states. There is even a greater need for leadership in those societies that have recently moved from an "authoritarian-pluralist" status to experiment with democracy—for example, Taiwan and South Korea.

In the light of these broad trends, the author takes a brief look at the problems of China's leadership during that nation's struggle to modernize. According to him, what distinguished Chiang Ching-kuo both from his father and from other elders of modern China was CCK's ability to recognize in the last years of his life that in a dynamic society genuine stability can be maintained only "when the system permits questioning, dissent, and political choice before discontent reaches an explosive level." The final compliment paid by Scalapino to CCK's leadership on Taiwan is as follows: "In sum, in choosing the appropriate priority, in selecting individuals capable of concentrating on that priority, in broadening the government's appeals to Taiwan's citizenry, and in timing the changes sufficiently well to make a reasonable degree of success possible, Chiang Ching-kuo fulfilled the requirements of the effective leader."

CHAPTER ONE

Historical Setting for the Rise of Chiang Ching-kuo

CHO-YUN HSU

Since the conference is organized around the personality of Chiang Ching-kuo, his role, and the legacy of his leadership, my assignment, to give the historical background of his time, ought to be organized around stages in his life. Chiang Ching-kuo's life can be divided into the following stages:

(1) Childhood 1910-1925
(2) Russian exile 1925-1937
(3) War years 1937-1949
(4) Serving his father in Taiwan 1949-1965
(5) His position as Minister of Defense and then as Premier 1965-1978
(6) His presidency 1978-1988.

I shall try to look at this period of the history of China with the same six divisions, discussing only historical background relevant to Chiang's life. As this is not a biography of Chiang Ching-kuo, no attempt is made to explain his personality.

(1) 1910-1925

In 1910, Chiang Ching-kuo was born. His childhood coincided with the early decades of the Republic, which was established in

1911. Warlords struggled to control China without reaching unification. In 1925, Sun Yat-sen, the only leader who enjoyed nationwide popularity, died. With his death, China lost the hope of peaceful reunification. The May Fourth Movement took place in 1919, indicating the influence of western civilization. In the southern provinces, especially in the vicinity of Shanghai, conflicts between the Chinese tradition and western values could be noticed in every aspect of life. The rise of socialist Russia after 1917 gave new hope to the new generation. Young intellectuals founded the Chinese Communist party in 1920-21; at that time its members collaborated with and infiltrated the new Kuomingtang party under Sun Yat-sen.

Chiang Ching-kuo was born at Feng-hua, a small market town not very far from Ning-po, from where one could easily sail to Shanghai. After 1913, his father, who joined Dr. Sun's revolutionary forces, was in exile to avoid arrest by the local authority, which sided with the northern warlords. Chiang Ching-kuo received his first schooling in 1916. The tutor was the same scholar who had taught Chiang Kai-shek some 15 years earlier. Chiang Kai-shek asked the teacher to tutor his son with the classical readings that were typical at that time. In 1921, Chiang Ching-kuo entered a new school located in the city, where he received modern education including mathematics, science, and geography. The father being constantly absent, Chiang Ching-kuo was extremely close to his mother, establishing a sentimental tie that was very important throughout his life. In 1922, Chiang Ching-kuo transferred to a primary school in Shanghai, and in 1923, he entered the Pu-tung Middle School, a prestigious private academy in a Shanghai suburb. On 30 May 1925, Shanghai workers protested against the special privileges of the foreign powers and their imperialism in China. This led to a bloody confrontation between Chinese workers and the police forces of foreign powers in Shanghai. Even though he was only 15 years old, Chiang Chink-kuo with many other youths joined the mass of angry Chinese to protest the May 30th Incident. He was dismissed by the school authority. Subsequently, he left for Peking, where he intended to learn French, yet ended being arrested because of his participation in another student protest in the capital of the War-lord government.[1]

Schools, even the middle schools, in which students were generally a few years older than ninth and tenth graders in the United States today, often were breeding grounds for an entire generation of socialist revolutionaries. Meanwhile, the sense of crisis associated with the encroachment of foreign powers upon China stimulated many young Chinese to adopt a position of ardent nationalism. It is in this historical context that Chiang Ching-kuo, riding on the tide of the times, developed strong patriotism in his middle school years. His decision to go to Russia was made in the mood shared by numerous Chinese youths because Russia was seen as supporting the Chinese position and aiding China in the struggle against the encroachment of the Capitalist powers.[2]

(2) 1925-1937

In Chinese history, the decade 1928-1937 was the period of Kuomingtang domination. It was also the period of Chiang Kai-shek's rise to the pinnacle of power. China was at least nominally united, although Chiang Kai-shek could directly govern only a limited area of China. The KMT party mechanism, copied from the model of Lenin's disciplined Bolsheviks, actually never reached the same level of discipline and organized solidarity, probably because of its much too rapid expansion. This period has often been regarded as the Golden Decade of the Republic. In reality, the process of reorganization and reintegration of China did not have a chance to run its full course.

Chiang Ching-kuo, during this eventful period, experienced 11 years of hardship in Russia until returning to China in 1937. There was speculation that he took the trip as a hostage, dispatched by Chiang Kai-shek to secure Russian support for his own rise in the KMT power-struggle in the heyday of the influence of the Communist International.[3] Chiang Ching-kuo himself, however, indicated that he made this decision by his own will when he was in Peking, where cooperation between the KMT and the Communist International created an atmosphere of warm friendship between China and Russia. The young Chiang Ching-kuo was friendly with Li Ta-chao, the founding father of the Chinese Communist party, and joined some 90 Chinese youths to leave for Russia to attend the

Sun Yat-sen University. After less than two years in the Sun Yat-sen University, Chiang Ching-kuo began to experience terrorism under Stalin. He was accused of Trotskyism, a faith to which he admitted to having been attracted. Meanwhile, Chiang Kai-shek broke away from the KMT leftists. Relations between Russia and China turned sour. Indeed, Chiang Ching-kuo then was virtually denied the chance of returning to China.

In the subsequent years, from 1928 until 1933, Chiang Ching-kuo had one job after another. He served in the Russian army, worked as an apprentice in an electrical plant, labored on a collective farm, and finally was exiled to a mine in the remote Ural region. In 1933 he was assigned to work in a factory making heavy machinery in the Ural region, where he met a Russian girl whom he married in 1935. During these years, the relationship between China and Russia was constantly in severe tension. In 1937, the imminent Japanese invasion, however, pulled Russia and China closer. For the sake of pleasing Chiang Kai-shek, Stalin released Chiang Ching-kuo. By then, Chiang Ching-kuo had spent 12 years in Russia. However, China also had witnessed tremendous changes. His father was an undisputed leader, yet was also very isolated from the people, confined by the dictatorship he built for himself.[4]

Reshaping the Chinese civilization after the western model picked up momentum in the decade after the sweeping influence of the May Fourth Movement that took place in 1919. It resulted in the emergence of a new group of western-educated intellectuals. Many of this new cultural and social elite advocated the values of liberalism, democracy, and scientism. Iconoclasm crushed the remnant of the traditional culture. The confrontation between xenophobic nostalgia and the mood of westernization finally created an enduring split among Chinese intellectuals. The KMT was caught in the middle of this crossfire. However, Japan's occupation of Manchuria and her subsequent intrusion in North China and the Shanghai region added more fuel to the growing patriotism, which eventually united the entire nation to fight for the very survival of China. Meanwhile, Chiang Kai-shek established an authoritarian government which was to cost him the support of intellectuals.

Allowed to go back to China, Chiang Ching-kuo probably found that the China he returned to appeared enormously different from the China he had left behind some 12 years before. The most significant mood of that time appeared to be a strong upsurge of patriotism and sense of emergency. Very soon China was plunged into a long, dragged out, and exhausting war against a massive Japanese invasion.

(3) 1937-1949

The war, which lasted eight years, ruined China completely. The effort of industrialization that had barely started in the coastal regions of China was abruptly interrupted. The besieged Chinese inland provinces were too exhausted to carry on the seemingly hopeless war. This was further complicated by the ceaseless struggles between the KMT and the Chinese Communist party forces who had been only nominally absorbed by the KMT as independent divisions of the government troops.

Chiang Ching-kuo's first assignment that made him widely recognized as a capable organizer was the position of commissioner in southern Kiangsi, which previously was an early base of the CCP Soviet. Southern Kiangsi, during much of the war, was cut off from the inland provinces where Chiang Kai-shek had built his wartime powers. Kiangsi was probably one of the last bastions along the periphery of the formerly prosperous coastal regions. It was a twilight area where every bit of ambivalence existed: old, rural-based, local military bands coexisted side by side with the socialist experiment launched by a young magistrate who had been endowed with discretionary powers to maintain this narrow passage between the backlands of the coastal regions and the vast underdeveloped inland provinces.

In 1939 Japanese invaded deeper into China, and much of the Kiangsi province was lost to the invader. In March of 1939, Chiang Ching-kuo was dispatched to work in Kiangsi. He was appointed to several positions concurrently: the commissioner of South Kiangsi, the magistrate of the Kan County, and the commandant of new recruits of the Kiangsi province. The area under his administration was the remainder of the entire Kiangsi province. It consists of 11 counties and a population of a little over one million. The provincial governor left Chiang Ching-kuo completely free to develop his programs. Chiang Ching-kuo put forth two Three-year Plans to build a "New South Kiangsi" with five goals: everyone has a job, everyone has food, everyone is clothed, everyone is housed, and everyone is educated. He cleared up banditry, gambling, prostitution, and the opium problem. In South Kiangsi, paved roads formed a network for transportation; schools provided primary education; "people's factories" were organized in the countryside; public stores served as retailing centers. Chiang Ching-kuo indeed tried to put some of his socialist ideas into practice. It ought to be noticed that his policies of maintenance of social order by means of cleaning up banditry, prostitution, etc., suppressed the influence of local leaders, some of whom had bullied in this inland area for a long time. All these behaviors actually also were typical in the tradition of Confucian "model officials." Therefore, it is not surprising that Chiang Ching-kuo was affectionately called by the Southern Kiangsi people "Chiang the Blue Sky," a nickname traditionally given to the incorrupt officials who brought "bright days" to the people.[5]

On the other hand, Chiang Ching-kuo's Russian background and his association with the leftist friends who worked for him as staff provoked much suspicion among the rightists around his father in Chungking. There was a rumor that the young Chiang was actually a practicing communist. Indeed, Chiang Ching-kuo must have been ideologically influenced by socialism. Nevertheless, his exposure to Confucian education and the great influence of heros in the Chinese tradition must also have had some impact upon his behavior. After all, ever since his returning from Russia, he had received intensive tutoring in Confucian education until he received the Kiangsi assignment. Cheng Kuo-fan's letter, Chu Hsi's essays, and the Family Instruction of Chu Po-lu were the principal ideas for him to study. It may not be sheer coincidence that in the farewell speech (October 1944), Chiang Ching-kuo told the Kiangsi people that he wished them to continue his unfinished work toward a society in which at least everyone could have a job and every household could have sufficient food in storage. He quoted as his dream the sentence "let the youth be nurtured, the grownup be employed, the old be taken care of" from the Confucian utopia of Great Peace. He also asked the people to manage their household and to behave themselves by following the Family Instruction of Chu Po-lu.[6] Thus Chiang Ching-kuo seems to have made great a effort to reconcile the socialism that inspired him to leave for Russia and the Confucian utopia that he had aspired to create since receiving a traditional education in childhood, and again after he returned to China.

The Kiangsi years were a very crucial period in Chiang Ching-kuo's life. There he developed the style of a populist politician, making policy decisions by directly feeling the mood of people and directly involving them in the implementation of policies. He cast aside the bureaucratic structure of formal government by installing rather innovative measures. Meanwhile, the high-tide of patriotism stimulated by the Japanese invasion and the sense of urgency about mobilizing the entire nation to preserve national independence made him, like many others of his time, believe that a strong national leadership was of paramount importance. This conviction was greatly reinforced by the killing of his mother by Japanese bombardment in December 1939. Due to the extremely close sentimental bond between mother and son, he swore to demand blood payment to clear the blood debt.[7] It is public knowledge that even in later days, after he assumed leadership in Taiwan, he was always reluctant to receive Japanese visitors. At any rate, the Kiangsi years determined that Chiang Ching-kuo would operate in Chinese politics in a style very different from that of his father and his contemporaries, most of whom tended to rely upon the national elite and formal government structure to govern.

The second half of the war period witnessed a virtually complete disintegration of the war-exhausted China. The economy suffered run-away inflation. Suspicions between the intellectuals and the government of Chiang Kai-shek radicalized the former and alienated the latter. Chiang Kai-shek had lost the mandate of the people even before Mao picked it up after the war was over.

In 1944, the frustrated Chiang Kai-shek decided to set up a program to train his own followers. A young cadets school was founded within the framework of the Youth Corps of Three People's Principles. Chiang Ching-kuo was called back from Kiangsi to work as the director of studies of this new school; its president was Chiang Kai-shek himself. Two hundred ninety-seven students were recommended by local chapters of the Youth Corps to receive one-year training in Chungking. This school was a cadet training ground rather than an academy, somewhat resembling the Sun Yat-sen University, which Chiang Ching-kuo had attended in Russia. Much of the curriculum was intensive study of the thought of Sun Yat-sen and Chiang Kai-shek, although prominent professors from the Central University were also invited to give series of lectures on philosophy, history, mathematics, English, and Chinese classics. The discipline was as tough and harsh as it would be in a military academy. Obviously Chiang Ching-kuo introduced to this school a style of discipline which he had experienced in Russia.[8] Again, Chiang Ching-kuo tried to combine Leninist revolutionary method and Neo-Confucian traditional ethics to rear a group of followers who were to be loyal to his father personally and committed to the KMT ideology. These students became his personal asset in later days. Many of them, including Li Huan, who recently served the premier of Taiwan, stayed with Chiang Ching-kuo even after they joined the Youth Corps School.

Chiang Ching-kuo did not have an opportunity to carry on this training program for a second year, as the Japanese surrendered in 1945. Chiang Ching-kuo was soon dispatched to Russia to negotiate a new Sino-Russian Treaty with Stalin and then assigned to negotiate the restoration of Chinese administration over Manchuria after the Russian occupation. Throughout his life, he recruited groups of followers to work for him. The graduates of the Youth Corps School, however, remained his most trusted ones.

Civil war after the Japanese War was a sequel to a process of disintegration which had already started in, say, 1940. In the five-year civil war after 1945, rural China defeated urban, modernized, coastal China. This was not because the people made a free choice between these two options. The opportunity to build a modern China in the coastal cities by the effort of industrialization and adoption of western civilization had been spoiled by the Japanese invasion. It is an irony that Mao Zedong, who claimed to launch a socialist revolution, actually gained his strength by converting many of the traditional elements in the rural area into forces that would be at his disposal. Illiterate peasants were his most crucial source of power. An economy organized in backland villages, as it had been there for centuries, managed to withstand the destructive effects of modern warfare.[9]

It was in the last ten years of the period under discussion that Chiang Ching-kuo learned firsthand of the difficulties of his father's government, and of the bitterness of defeat as well. His loyalty to and admiration for his father made him the most trusted aide of the often betrayed Generalissimo. Repeatedly, Chiang Ching-kuo was assigned the most difficult missions: to negotiate with Stalin, to regain control of Manchuria, and to restore economic order in Shanghai. He failed in all these assignments. Nevertheless, no one, even his enemies, held him responsible for the failure, because all these missions were initially impossible.

This was a period of political internship for Chiang Ching-kuo. His father was the most dominant figure in China. Nevertheless, he was by no means unchallenged. Facing the options of establishing a city-based modern state or concentrating power in the head of state for the sake of focusing resources on a single goal, Chiang Kai-shek chose the latter. The nationwide sense of crisis that called for the union of all Chinese, of course, provided him with much justification for launching a personal dictatorship. The young Chiang Ching-kuo, baptized politically in this period, could hardly have developed along paths other than those into which Chiang Kai-shek put him. In a time when China lost many of her elite, Chiang Ching-kuo managed to emerge as the combination of a worthy young idealist and a shrewd ringleader who began to build a group of his own followers as he repeatedly recruited young students to join him in undertaking various missions during and after the Japanese War years. Thus, in the decade of setbacks for China's development toward modernity, Chiang Ching-kuo launched his own political career with fortunate opportunities not only to gain experience but also to gather around himself a good number of followers. It must be noted, however, that he and his followers were not related to the circle of cultural elite trained in the coastal campuses. Mutual suspicions between Chiang's group and the cultural elite, unfortunately, were not eliminated until the 1970s.

(4) 1949-1965

China fell into the hands of the CCP, and Chiang Kai-shek moved his government to Taiwan. This last province of the republic had been recently returned to China after 50 years of Japanese occupation. During the colonial period, Taiwan had built to some degree a foundation of industrialization and urbanization. In the war years, however, the colonial Taiwan also suffered economic drainage in order to support the Japanese war machine. In addition, American bombardment ruined its railways, highways, and much of its industries. Misunderstandings between the Taiwanese and the provincial authority appointed by Chiang Kai-shek eventually exploded into massive violence on 28 February 1947. When Chiang Kai-shek moved to Taiwan, he actually had in hand a battered economy and a situation where mutual suspicion between mainlanders and the local island population was fermenting hidden hostilities.

On the other hand, in the 1950s, although urbanization had begun, the Taiwan population was still basically a rural one. The Japanese for 50 years had not nurtured the development of local leadership. The local elite fared well only in limited professions, such as medicine. One of the most valuable legacies the Japanese gave to Taiwan, however, was a universal primary education system and authoritative rule by law. The KMT government, therefore, found in Taiwan a law-abiding and relatively literate population. The government faced little challenge from local social forces, as they lacked leadership. In contrast, during the mainland days, the KMT often had to accommodate the resistance of local interests, which were strong enough to block any reform the government intended to put forward. Hence, with the assistance of Sino-American joint organization (the JCRR—Joint Commission of Rural Reconstruction) and its veteran agricultural experts, the KMT administration under Ch'en Ch'eng successfully completed an islandwide agricultural reform, which combined the land-to-the-tiller program and a technological Green Revolution by modernizing farming techniques. Village prosperity and the revival of industrialization helped Taiwan take the first step toward its spectacular economic growth.

Another task the KMT tried to accomplish was to rebuild a sense of Chinese nationalism so that the local population, who had been separated from China for half a century, were sentimentally reintegrated into the nation of China.[10] The KMT government was forced by the United States to give up any attempt at recovering the Chinese mainland in return for American protection. Nevertheless, an emphasis on Chinese-ness and the claim of status as the continuation of the legitimate government over all of China were viewed as the justification of its very existence. As a result, a rather clumsy and outdated government structure had to be maintained at the expense of extending economic reform toward political reforms.

Chiang Ching-kuo served in this period in various roles. His principal functions, however, were to stabilize the situation by means of organizing a military commissar system, an intelligence service, and a youth corps. Stability was the key concept of the 1950s and early 1960s. Chiang Ching-kuo in this period was one of the major organizers in the KMT camp. His father would not have felt comfortable to see any other political figure have numerous followers. Being the most trusted person, Chiang Ching-kuo managed to expand his circle of followers in a number of official or semi-official capacities.

A controversial issue arose in Chiang Ching-kuo's role of organizing a network of intelligence. Having learned during his Russian years the use of a secret agency for controlling people, Chiang Ching-kuo as early as his early political career in Kiangsi had organized a KGB-style network of intelligence to gather information by planting in various posts a few of his trusted followers who would report to him any deviation and corruption of conduct of officials.[11] In the early decades of reestablishing his father's governance, he was responsible for reorganizing into an integrated body several previously independent networks of intelligence which had served his father in the mainland days. Such a secret service could be helpful in gaining some social and political stability. It might also be instrumental in the competition for political supremacy among various factions of the government and party structures and among contenders for the second highest positions under Chiang Kai-shek. Chiang Ching-kuo indeed benefitted from having such a weapon for the struggle against other major figures in the higher echelon of Taiwan power circles. Nevertheless, he also had to bear the adverse consequence of being regarded as ruthless and reactionary, alienated from the intellectuals, and distrusted by other members of the Chiang Kai-shek government. Furthermore, the tarnished image of a ruthless leader using the intelligence service to gain power remained unchanged until the very last years of his life.

Also in this period, Chiang Ching-kuo in another assignment learned to seek new sources of talents. The hope of returning to the mainland by military reconquest had faded away. The soldiers who had come to Taiwan with the KMT government gradually aged. Chiang Kai-shek launched a large-scale reorganization of the oversized armed forces. Chiang Ching-kuo's assignment was to settle the retired veterans in the public construction projects. For so doing, he ceaselessly visited Taiwan's countryside and the inland mountainous regions. He thus got acquainted with local conditions.

After 1951 he founded tens of farms to settle the aged soldiers and organized a large engineering corps to carry on public construction, mainly the cross-island highway and numerous highdams for power plants. He thus had the opportunity to be in contact with agricultural experts, engineers, and other technocratic personalities. As Y. S. Tsiang recalled, Chiang Ching-kuo for the first time realized the value of modern science and technology and began to appreciate the service of the intellectuals as he and Tsiang, then a staff expert in the Joint Commission of Rural Reconstruction, made hundreds of trips to view the horticultural experiments in developing new species and the sites of dams to admire the precision of engineering surveys.[12] Such experiences were indispensable for Chiang Ching-kuo's appreciation of the capability of the modern education experts who could render valuable services for economic development.

In summary, Taiwanese society at that time lacked any kind of intermediate social groups to integrate the society and the state. There was neither a layer of strong social elite coming from the mainland to Taiwan, nor a layer of local leadership taking root in the island. Chiang Ching-kuo's expansion of influence, therefore, faced little challenge. The monolithic power structure of an authoritarian state completely overwhelmed Taiwan's development. Even economic development was initiated and guarded by the state. The momentum for change, however, was gathering as economic growth progressed.

(5) 1965-1978

Chiang Ching-kuo served in two positions in this period, first as the minister of defense (1965-72), and then as premier (1972-78). Actually, he had taken over from his father much of the responsibility in daily routines as well as making policies.

Chiang Ching-kuo began to change some aspects of his political behavior. Because he often moved about freely among ordinary folk and gathered first-hand information about people's livelihood by chatting with them, he gradually moved away from the influence of the intelligence network. It seemed that he realized that a national leadership must be built upon services rendered by all kinds of talents in numerous aspects of state affairs. Thus as the minister of defense, he once openly declared that he would employ those who had newly joined him rather than old-timers, and those who were formerly distant rather than the close ones.[13] This statement probably was meant to explain to his old associates in the military and intelligence circles that he needed to gain the confidence of people in other sectors of state affairs because he had to broaden his scope of operation and shift his attention especially to economic development.

Indeed, during the days he served in the Cabinet, he gathered around him a good number of technocrats who were to be the national leaders, such as Sun Yun-suan, Y. S. Tsiang, S. T. Tao, Chu-yu Chao, etc. With the assistance of the technocrats, Chiang Ching-kuo organized an extremely efficient team of assistants who helped him modernize the armed forces, not only in equipment but also in organization. In 1973 he launched major public construction projects, including an island-wide highway system, hydraulic and nuclear power plants, heavy industrial complexes, new or expanded harbors, tax-free industrial parks, and other projects which were related to development of infrastructures necessary for an economic take-off. The completion of the Ten Major Projects brought Taiwan's economy to a new level. Of primary importance is that planners, engineers, technicians, and workers who were involved in these projects gained valuable experience and confidence. Twelve more projects were started right after the completion of the Ten for the purpose of sustaining further economic growth.[14] Much of the most significant infrastructure for the advancement of Taiwan's economy was built in this period, and valuable human resources, including a large number of skilled laborers and field and production line technicians, were trained. Additionally, the future middle class of Taiwan began to appear in this period.

Taiwan in the 1960s had gathered sufficient momentum to move rapidly toward a modern economy based upon manufacturing and export trade. An effective combination of authoritarianism and technocracy guided the public as well as the private economy to form capital, to develop technology, and to use its high-quality labor force. Economic growth was the keynote of this period.[15]

Notable changes took place. In 1965 American aid, crucial in the early stages of Taiwan development, was phased out. Nevertheless, the annual rate of growth after 1964 often surpassed the original targeted figures, reaching 9.1 percent in the 1960s, and nearly 10 percent in the 1970s. In 1973 the Gross National Product (GNP) reached $9.39 billion, while in 1952 it had been a mere $1.2 billion. After 1973, Taiwan continued to enjoy a trade surplus with all nations except Japan. The per capita income was $467 in 1963 and $702 in 1974.[16] The literacy rate increased from 57 percent in 1950 to 89.5 percent in 1978. The percentage of high school graduates increased from 10 percent to 42.6 percent in the same period. The demographic distribution ratio of the rural population changed from 60 percent in 1950 to 22 percent in 1978 (tabulated from yearbooks of the Republic of China). As Tables I and II show, the rural sector of the economy had given way to the industrial ones, and as Tables III and IV show, the value of industrial output and international trade increased rapidly in this period. Taiwan was experiencing a permanent change in these decades.

Taiwanese society experienced drastic diversification in its composition. New leaders were created. New social groups were formed. Taiwanese society was not a mechanically associated structure anymore, in Durkheim's terminology; it was reshaped into a modern entity. International trade and the massive influx of students returning from abroad, by introducing all kinds of value systems found in various religions, ideological systems, and fashions of thinking and behavior, made an important impact on Taiwan. It then had to accept the reality of plurality of values, which, of course, was a counterpoise to the monolithic authoritarianism of the KMT political system.

Taiwan also had to face repeated blows to its very chance of survival as an autonomous entity. In 1972, the People's Republic of China replaced the Republic of China as a member of the United Nations. Subsequently, Taiwan lost diplomatic recognition as a member of the international community. People in Taiwan experienced unprecedented challenge. It was the economic strength they had built in the past decades that gave them the only means to cope with these adverse conditions. The identity of China, however, suffered from the severe doubt about the very legitimacy of the entire political structure.

(6) 1978-1988

Chiang Ching-kuo assumed his own term of presidency. After decades of a supporting role, he moved to the front of the stage. In this decade, he steered Taiwan through the difficult, choppy waters of rejections abroad and protests at home. In 1979, the United States officially recognized the Peking government. Taiwan survived, in a not-so-honored and often-embarrassed international status, as a corporate body under the American Taiwan Relations Act. Ironically, foreign investment flowed to Taiwan in spite of the seeming uncertainty of Taiwan's status, as shown in Figure 1. Miraculously, Taiwan's economy continued to thrive. In 1980 Taiwan had a GNP of $40.3 billion, a per capita average of $2,100. In 1988, the GNP was $119 billion, and the per capita average $6,053. A small island of merely 20 million people, Taiwan held more than 10 percent of the world reserves of foreign exchange.

It should be noticed, moreover, that wealth was rather fairly shared by a majority of the people. As Chiang Ching-kuo and his ministers repeatedly declared, the goal of economic development was the fulfillment of the ancient ideal of making people equally share the wealth. The income ratio of the highest and the lowest 20 percent wage-earners was 15.1 in 1952, 5.33:1 in 1964, and 4.69:1 in 1987. Compared with other newly industrialized countries, Taiwan fared very well.[17] The goal of reaching a relatively fair distribution of wealth is indeed part of the Confucian ideal as well as that of Sun Yat-sen. It still takes some policy to materialize the vision. Chiang Ching-kuo in his populist approach often would mingle with the ordinary people. He therefore did have a better knowledge of the livelihood of the people, especially that of the poor sector of the society. In 1972, he launched nine projects to revitalize the rural economy. The emphasis was upon taking care of the welfare of farmers, salt producers, and fishermen, the three professions of least incomes. A rural-area network of medical service was also set up at the same time.[18]

Domestically, political reform was then recognized as the most crucial issue on the agenda. Chiang Ching-kuo was fully aware of the significance of reorientation of the national goal. He openly proclaimed that after 40 years residing in Taiwan, he, himself, had become one of the "Taiwanese." Social diversification had actually reached the level of social disintegration. Numerous social groups all sought their own interests. As Table V shows, the number and membership of civic organizations grew rapidly after 1977. As a sociologist noted, a total of 18 social movements had emerged in Taiwan to make claims on the state in the 1980s. They ranged from the consumers' movement to the women's movement, from the minority rights to the environmental protection movement, from the farmer and labor movement to that of the handicapped and the disadvantaged. The frequency of their emergence rapidly increased: one in 1980, three in 1982, one in 1983, one in 1986, seven in 1987, and four in 1988.[19] A good majority of these social movements emerged in the last years of Chiang Ching-kuo's presidency. The most obvious protesters, of course, were the political dissenters who challenged the single-party political structure. In 1986, a new Democratic Progress party was formed as the only serious non-

KMT political organization, and the political atmosphere was forever changed.

Chiang Ching-kuo not only tolerated the new opposition party's participation in a general election, but he even moved further to lift the curfew under martial law, which had been imposed upon the people of Taiwan for 40 years. The last two years of his presidency witnessed drastic changes in Taiwan's politics. Through a series of interactions between the KMT and opposition forces, Taiwan strode toward fuller democratization. Violent mass movements appeared almost daily in the news. The government also often surprised observers by launching political reforms, allowing more space for political opposition.

Any further democratization, in the very unusual case of Taiwan, was tangled with the issue of permanent independence from China. The issue was further complicated by the continuous overtures extended by the Peking government to invite Taiwan's return to China. Chiang Ching-kuo once again surprised observers by allowing people to visit relatives in the mainland. Thus, contacts and communications across the Taiwan strait added a new variable to the demand for localization and democratization.

This highly charged political atmosphere was not the only concern of the Taiwanese in this period. Inflation and an overheated economy ushered in a series of economic factors that could change the direction of Taiwan's economic development in the future. All these indeed would be issues which Taiwan must face in the future. However, in Taiwan an entrepreneurial Chinese population had testified to the world that China could be brought to modernity if Chinese were given a relatively peaceful time to work. In Taiwan, during this decade, there emerged a pluralistic society. The private sector of the economy exceeded the public sector. Individualism replaced collectivism in the mood of thinking. Society began to check and to seek for balances with the state, which thus faced unprecedented challenge.

* * * * *

Chiang Ching-kuo died in 1988. The Taiwan of the 1980s had been completely different from that of the 1950s. The task of reorientation of Taiwan, and, even of China, was started by Chiang Ching-kuo's own hand; from a historical perspective, however, this change had been prepared by three generations of Chinese ever since the last century. Chiang Ching-kuo lived through the entire course of continuous effort of reorganizing China, including all its political, economic, and cultural dimensions. The historical development took a long and winding course, interrupted in the middle of several setbacks, especially the Japanese War and the CCP's revolution. In Taiwan, at least one part of the Chinese population managed to have pushed the historical development quite a few steps toward their longtime targeted goal. Chiang Ching-kuo, in his last years, which were the years of his own leadership, had taken within his grasp the active role of helping Taiwan make remarkable strides.

Chiang Ching-kuo was brought up in an atmosphere of highly charged patriotism. To him total dedication to the cause of making China free from foreign encroachment was not empty talk. His early education, as well as its reinforcement after his returning from Russia, also made him identify his own goal as that of serving China. The memory of hardship in Russia probably led him to even closer attachment to China, an image that he often associated with a love of his own mother. The life experience of a plain household in a small inland marketing town left a deep imprint in his populist approach to political behavior. A socialist education in Russia simply reinforced his inclination to populism. He could have followed a political path very different from that of his father. Nevertheless, the traditional Chinese Confucian education probably made him put filial piety as his first duty, and therefore he gradually became a confidant and then a successor of his father. Due to his populism, he was originally hostile to the intellectuals, especially the Western-educated ones of upperclass families. Likewise, he originally hated bureaucracy. However, because he had to be a part of the politics of his father, he had to inherit the bureaucracy and even learned to play the game of factional struggle on behalf of his father as well as his own behalf. His association with the intelligence service therefore, for a long time, became his base of power as well as his liability. Chiang Ching-kuo did not begin to recruit technocrats into his own circle until he was involved in economic development. In his last years he made efforts to depend upon the technocrats who served in his government to create the economic miracle that Taiwan achieved. However, he never developed happy relationships with intellectuals in general. His tolerance of Taiwan's democratization was a shrewd recognition of the inevitable rather than a promotion of the cause of democracy as an ideal. The result, of course, is that Taiwan headed toward democratization after economic growth had reached such a level that the civil society became sufficiently strong to demand political reform. Chiang Ching-kuo gave his life to work for China; he also received proper recognition of his merit.

TABLE I

Agricultural Population and Agriculture's Contribution to Net Domestic Product

Year	Agriculture Population as Percent of Total Population	Agriculture's Contribution to NDP
1952	52.4	35.9
1957	49.4	31.7
1962	48.0	29.2
1967	44.7	23.8
1972	38.9	14.1
1977	33.1	12.5
1982	26.4	9.2
1985	21.5	7.0

Source: Council for Economic Planning and Developing, ROC, *Taiwan Statistical Data Book*, 1986, pp. 39 and 63.

From: Joseph P. L. Jiang, "The Development of Social Pluralism and Political Liberalization in the Republic of China on Taiwan," in Bernard T, K. Joei (ed.), *Taiwan in Transition: Political Development and Economic Prosperity* (Taipei: Tamkang University, 1988), p. 22.

TABLE II

Composition of Exports in Taiwan 1961-1985 (%)

Period	Agricultural Products	Processed Ag. Products	Industrial Products
1961-65	15.8	40.0	44.2
1966-70	12.8	19.7	67.5
1971-75	6.5	10.1	83.4
1976-80	4.7	6.2	89.1
1981-85	1.8	5.1	93.1

Source: *Taiwan Statistical Data Book*, 1987 CEPD, Taipei.

From: Peter C. Y. Chou, "Economic Liberalization in Taiwan (ROC) and Its Implications for Pacific Development" in Bernard Joei, *op. cit.*, p. 120.

TABLE III

Percentage Share of Export (X) and Import (M) in the GNP (Y)

Period	X/Y	M/Y	X+M/Y
1961-65	16.64	19.80	36.44
1966-70	24.56	21.60	46.16
1971-75	41.32	40.72	82.04
1976-80	51.00	48.26	99.26
1981-85	53.84	45.44	99.28

Source: *Taiwan Statistican Data Book*, 1987 CEPD, Taipei.

From: Peter C. Y. Chou, *op. cit.*, p. 120.

TABLE IV

Taiwan's Growth Rates of Selected Economic Indicators: 1953-1985 (%)

Period	Real GNP	Real per Capita GNP	Exports	Imports	Industrial Production	Consumer Prices
1953-62	7.5	4.0	19.5	17.0	11.7	8.7
1963-72	10.8	8.1	29.9	23.5	18.5	2.9
1973-86	7.9	6.2	19.8	17.1	9.6	8.4

Source: *Taiwan Statistical Data Book*, 1987 edition, Council for Economic Planning and Development, Taipei, p. 2.

From: Charles H. C. Kao, "Taiwan Development Experience: Lessons on Perspectives," in Bernard Joei, *op. cit.*, p. 130.

TABLE V

Number and Membership of Civic Organizations

Year	Number of Organizations	Individuals	Members (1,000)	Groups
1952	2,560	1,316		2,844
1957	4,194	1,759		7,028
1962	5,217	2,338		9,287
1967	5,296	2,496		18,936
1972	6,173	3,398		22,062
1977	7,476	3,902		34,600
1982	9,060	5,420		50,949
1985	10,482	6,452		101,036

Source: Council for Economic Planning and Development, ROC, *Taiwan Statistical Data Book*, 1986, p. 297.

From: Joseph P. L. Jiang, *op.cit.*, p. 22.

Figure 1:

Direct Foreign Investment in Taiwan
1960-1986

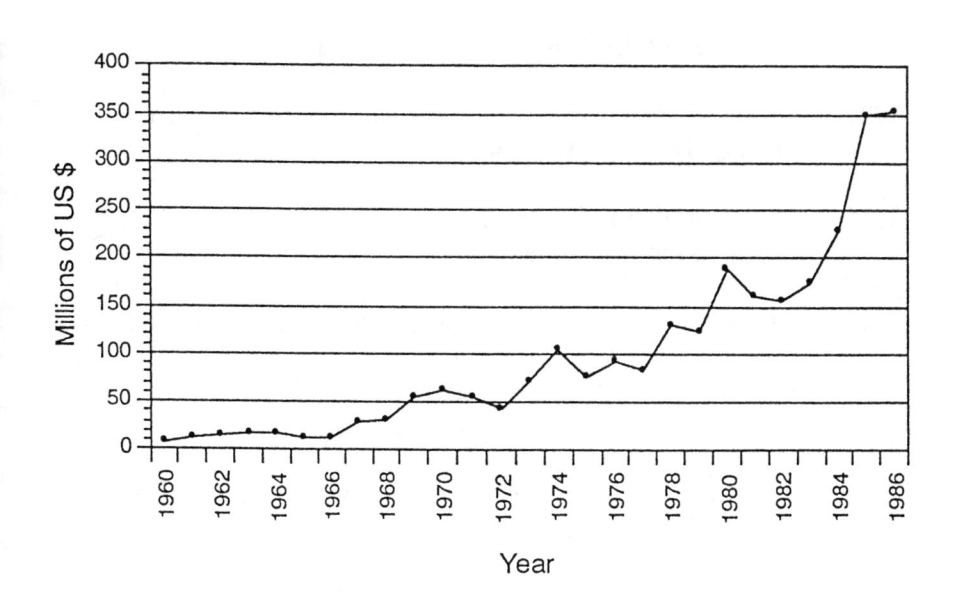

From: Chi Schive, "Direct Foreign Investment in Taiwan" in Bernard Joei, op. cit., p. 143.

APPENDIX: CHIANG CHING-KUO CHRONICLES

1910   Chiang Ching-kuo was born in Hsi-kou, Feryhua, to Chiang Kai-shek and Mao Fu-mei.

1916   Entered Wu-shan Primary School, Hsi-kou.

1917   Tutored by Ku Ching-lien, the teacher of his father.

1920   Tutored by Wang Ou-sheng.

1921   Transferred to Lung-tsin School, Fenghua.

1922   Transferred to Wan-chu School, Shanghai. Wang Ou-sheng also went with him.

1924   Graduated from Wan-chu School. Then entered Pu-tung Middle School, Shanghai.

1925   Expelled from Pu-tung Middle School, and transferred to Preparatory School of Foreign Languages, Peking. In October, took off to Russia to enroll at Sun Yat-sen University.

1928   Transferred to Leningrad Red Army Central Military and Political Academy.

1930   Graduated from Military and Political Academy, and entered Lenin College.

1931   Dispatched to work in an Electrical Machinery Plant in Moscow suburb.

1933   Sent to work in state farms in Siberia, Ural Mountain region, and in a power plant.

1934	Promoted to station chief of the power plant.
1935	Married with Fanni.
1937	Returned to China; joined KMT. Restudied Chinese classics, Tsing Kuo-fan's correspondences, and Sun Yat-sen's works.
1938	Appointed deputy director of security office, Kiang-hsi Province, and concurrently the commandant of New Recruits of Kiang-hsi.
1939	Concurrently served as commissioner of the fourth district of Kianghsi and the country magistrate of Kan-hsien.
1940	Assigned to be in charge of the Kianghsi branch of the Youth Corps of Three Principles (of San Yat-sen).
1941	Dispatched to visit the Northwestern Provinces. Later, appointed political commissar of the newly formed Youth Army Expedition Headquarters.
1943	Appointed a member of the Kianghsi Provincial Council.
1944	Appointed director of studies, Central Cadet Academy of the Youth Corps.
1945	Assigned the mission to negotiate recovery of Manchuria from Russian occupation.
1946	Visited Moscow to negotiate with Stalin on a Treaty of Sino-Russo Friendship and the recovery of Manchuria.
1948	Assigned mission to control runaway inflation of Shanghai.
1949	Appointed to head Taiwan KMT chapter, and to prepare for the retreat of Chiang Kai-shek to Taiwan.

1950	Helped his father reorganize KMT. Served as political commissar Ministry of Defense. Commanded the withdrawal of armed forces stationed in the Chekiang offshore islands.
1952	Organized the Anti-Communist Youth Corps.
1956	Took the assignment to settle the retired veterans.
1957	Elected to the KMT Standing Committee.
1958	Appointed minister without portfolio in Yen Chia-Kan's cabinet. Quemoy-Matsu bombardment.
1964	Served as deputy minister of defense.
1965	Served as minister of defense.
1970	Served as deputy prime minister and also head of commission on economic development.
1972-73	Served as prime minister. Ten Projects of Major Construction completed.
1974	Started 14 new economic and financial policies.
1975	Father Chiang Kai-shek died. Vice President Yen Chia-kan succeeded to presidency. Chiang Ching-kuo became the chairman of KMT.
1977	Announced 12 projects for consideration to follow the completion of the Ten Major Projects.
1978	Elected president of Republic of China.
1980	Announced new policies to improve rural economic conditions.

1984	Elected to his second term of the presidency. Lee Teng-hui elected as the vice president.
1985	Publicly declared that he had become a Taiwanese, and that no more Chiang family members would run for presidency.
1986	Declared that the curfew based on martial law was to be lifted and new political parties to be allowed to participate in political activities.
1987	The 40-years-old curfew was lifted (July). Citizens in Taiwan were allowed to visit Mainland China (November).
1988	13 January, Chiang Ching-kuo died of heart failure.

ENDNOTES

1. Martin Wilbur and Salie Lien-Hou, *Missionaries of Revolution: Soviet Advisors and Nationalist China, 1920-1927* (Cambridge: Harvard University Press, 1989), pp. 149-153.

2. Ibid., pp. 171-177.

3. Wang Yueh-hsi, "Mao Fu-mei and the Father and Son of the Chiangs' Family," *Chuan-chi Wen-hsueh* (Biographic Literature), 1989, no. 322, p. 125.

4. Chiang Ching-kuo, "My Days in the Soviet Union," ibid., 1989, no. 323, pp. 73-79. English version is in Ray S. Cline, *Chiang Ching-kuo Remembered: the Man and His Political Legacy* (Washington, D.C.: United States Global Strategy Council, 1989), Appendix, pp. 148-ff.

5. Ch'i Kuo-ju, "My Views on Chiang Ching-kuo's Ability in Judging and Employing People," *Chuan-chi Wen-hsueh*, 1989, no. 330, pp. 71-81.

6. Hsieh Jan-chih, "From Ma-chia Temple to Fu-hisn Pass," ibid., 1989, no. 320, p. 21.

7. Wang Yueh-hsi, *op. cit.*, pp. 134-135.

8. Hsieh Jan-chih, *op. cit.*, pp. 18-19. Cf. "A letter from Chang Tseng-chuan, " ibid., no. 321, p. 43.

9. The loss of the KMT to the CCP is too complicated an issue to be discussed here. For a summary, see Emmanuel C. Y. Hsu, *The Rise of Modern China* (New York: Oxford University Press, 1990), Chaps. 24,25.

10. Richard Wilson, *Learning to be Chinese: Political Socialization of Children in Taiwan* (Cambridge: MIT Press, 1970).

11. Chang Ling-ao, "Random Recollection of Chiang Ching-kuo's Schoolmates in Russia," *Chuan-chi wen-hsueh*, 1990, no. 332, p. 14.

12. Tsiang's conversation, 4/9/90.

13. Ch'i Kuo-ju, *op. cit.*, p. 76.

14. Hsu, *op. cit.*, pp. 906-909.

15. Walter Galenson (ed.), *Economic Growth and Structural Change in Taiwan: An Experiment in Social China* (Ithaca: Cornell University Press, 1979).

16. Hsu, *op. cit.*, pp. 754-755, 904.

17. Ibid., p. 905.

18. Wang, Cho-jung, "Mr. Chiang Ching-kuo and the Economic Development of Taiwan," in *Reminiscence about President Chiang Ching-kuo* (Taipei: Li-ming, 1988), pp. 244-248.

19. Michael Hsin-huang Hsiao, "Emerging Social Movements and the Rise of a Demanding Civil Society in Taiwan," a paper presented at the Conference on Democratization in the Republic of China, IIR, 9-11 January 1989, Taipei.

CHAPTER TWO

Chiang Ching-kuo's Decision for Political Reform

**ANDREW J. NATHAN
AND
HELENA V. S. HO**

In March 1986 President Chiang Ching-kuo launched a dramatic political reform which marked a shift from gradual liberalization under a regime of "soft authoritarianism" to the beginning of what seems to be a process of democratic transition.[1] To date, this process has achieved or facilitated, among other things, the lifting of martial law, the legalization of opposition parties, a smooth constitutional transition of political power after Chiang's death, a marked freeing up of the print media, and the invigoration of the electoral arena—all substantial moves in the direction of democracy.

This chapter seeks to analyze Chiang Ching-kuo's motives for launching the reform at the time that he did, in the context of the theory of democratic transitions. The focus on Chiang is appropriate because the available evidence (some of it reviewed in the section on "party renewal" below) supports the conventional wisdom that the reform decision was Chiang's and Chiang's alone. This does not gainsay the fact that he took the decision in response to conditions at home and abroad; it is these conditions and his response to them that this chapter seeks to analyze. But it is easier to identify these surrounding conditions than to figure out what

Chiang made of them. To the limited extent that we can clarify Chiang's calculations and motives, our findings will be of historical and biographical interest, enriching our understanding of the political goals and style of this little-known and elusive political leader, and to some extent helping us decipher his vision for Taiwan's future.

In addition, such an investigation has a contribution to make to theory. A reform leader's motives are only part of the total story of a political reform, but they are an important part of it from the perspective of the transitions literature, which tends to focus on elite motives and strategies.[2] We will argue that Taiwan's experience, like Spain's in the 1970s, fits into Alfred Stepan's "Path 4a" ("redemocratization initiated by the civilian or civilianized political leadership"), but that it also differs from Spain's in some interesting respects. Comparing this case to the model and to the similar case should help clarify both the Taiwan case and the theory.

The dating of the reforms from March 1986 refers to the meeting that month of the Third Plenum of the KMT's 12th Central Committee. Chiang, as party chairman, called on the delegates to make stepped-up progress towards the party's long-standing goal of constitutional democracy. Not much was accomplished on this task at the session, so in early April Chiang appointed a 12-man task force, which he charged with framing reform proposals to solve four specific issues: how to lift the ban on formation of new parties, how to lift martial law, how to revise the Taiwan Provincial Government Organization Law, and how to reform the Legislative Yuan and National Assembly.[3] The task force made its first report in June. In October, the president informed Katharine Graham of the *Washington Post* of his intention to lift the martial law decree and legalize opposition parties. Formal lifting of the martial law decree occurred in July 1987, followed by other reform measures. Meanwhile, in September 1986 the opposition had already formally established its own political party, which the regime tolerated even though it was at first still illegal.[4]

This chapter will not seek to analyze President Chiang's choice of reform tasks, because there was little ambiguity or controversy over what the initial steps of reform would involve when and if they were taken. Taiwan was ruled under a constitution promulgated in mainland China in 1947, modified by "Temporary Provisions" that had come into effect on that island in 1948 and under which various martial law provisions were enacted. Given the commitment of the ruling Kuomintang (KMT) since its founding to "constitutional government and democracy," the initial agenda for political reform inevitably involved lifting the martial law decree and moving toward fuller implementation of the constitution.[5] Given the rapid rate at which old mainland-elected members of the national representative bodies were dying off, "renewal" of these bodies was inescapably high on the agenda. And given the opposition's insistent and widely supported demand for more press freedom and more electoral competition, so too was removal of the bans on newspapers and new political parties. There was room for disagreement about the details of these steps and what would follow them, but most of these issues did not come up for decision until after Chiang Ching-kuo's death in January 1988.

Nor do we attempt to analyze the conditioning factors making this democratic transition possible. They have been elucidated by Tun-jen Cheng, among others. First, Taiwan had reached a socioeconomic level that fulfilled the precondition for democracy; e.g., high per-capita income, relatively equitable income distribution, high educational levels, and a high proportion of citizens identifying themselves as members of the middle class. Second, specific features of Taiwan's class structure helped make democratization easier: the lack of landlords and big capitalists and the cross-cutting nature of political and economic cleavages. Third, the regime's constitutionalist and prodemocratic ideology, strong liberal-technocrat faction, deep roots in society, and substantial legitimacy and organizational strength facilitated reform. Fourth, Cheng emphasizes the importance of elections and the pressure from a maturing opposition in encouraging the KMT to reform.

But, as Cheng points out, "The actual decisionmaking process of the democratic breakthrough in 1986 is yet to be studied."[6] This is the focus of our analysis. We cannot weigh the relative importance of the leader's decisions as against the permissive conditions, because such an evaluation, if it is possible at all, would require a broader study. We assume that socioeconomic conditions and leadership factors are both important in some way. Even if conditions are the most important of the two in determining whether a democratic transition will take place, political leadership is crucial in influencing the timing of the transition, its smoothness, the order in which transition measures are taken, and the type of institutional structure toward which the reform at least initially moves. In the case of Taiwan, socioeconomic conditions for democratization had been ripe for at least 10 or 15 years, and the domestic opposition and foreign critics had been pressing for change for an equal length of time, before Chiang Ching-kuo made his decision to allow the process to move forward.

It turns out that the question of why the leader acted when and as he did is hard to answer in Taiwan's case; this is probably why it remains the least studied aspect of the story. CCK (as he was often called) cultivated a populist image, but he kept his personality and his motivations to himself. The *Asian Wall Street Journal* reported in November 1987, "The reason for the democratic turn is a mystery. . . . Mr. Chiang is in no hurry to shed light on these events. He hasn't written about his life and has declined to cooperate with biographers. In answering written questions submitted by the Asian Journal, he ignored an invitation to talk about himself. . . ."[7] Chiang's public statements were usually couched in a hackneyed Confucian phraseology which—however sincerely he meant it, and we will argue that he probably did—tended to deter analysis. He listened to many different opinions, but even his close subordinates apparently did not know how he put the information together. Since he encouraged his aides to imitate his reticence in speaking both about him and about their roles with him,[8] even after his death those around him revealed relatively little about his thinking during the time the reform decision was made. As Tilman Durdin had written earlier, "The cult of concealment that surrounds the personal life of this shy and wary man . . . make [sic] him something of an unknown quantity to the world at large."[9]

We have scrutinized each factor that appears likely to have influenced his reform decision, examined how this influence might have worked, and marshalled whatever evidence is available to help clarify whether this factor really did play a role in his thinking. For ease of exposition we have ordered the factors roughly in narrowing concentric circles around Chiang, looking first at two international factors, then at two in the sphere of Taiwan, and finally at two pertaining to Chiang himself. In each case, we examine how the factor in question may have appeared to Chiang and may have influenced his decision. The ordering is meant to imply nothing about the relative importance of the factors, since we have no way to measure this.

Although the result of this analysis is inconclusive, we hope it gives a relatively plausible reconstruction of Chiang's motives and sharpens issues for further research, which might be conducted if more presidential papers become available or if further interviews can be carried out with President Chiang's colleagues and subordinates.

International Pressure

Martial law had long been an embarrassment to Taiwan in its international relations. For example, in a 1983 interview with *Der Spiegel*, President Chiang confronted a number of sharp questions. He was told, "Never before in modern history has there been a country as long under martial law as Taiwan." The interviewers asked when martial law would be lifted, and also "Why is Taiwan so slow in democratization?" The president's answers showed that he did not find it easy to answer such questions. As to martial law, he confessed, "This is indeed a dilemma," then stated both that martial law was needed to defend Taiwan from the communists and that its effect was extremely slight. On democracy, he argued that Taiwan was already quite democratic without an opposition party, but also acknowledged that "No political party can maintain its advantage forever if it does not reflect the public opinion and meet the people's demand."[10]

According to CCK's long-term chief secretary, Wang Chia-hua, Chiang, even before becoming president, was frequently embarrassed in this way. When foreign visitors asked him, as Taiwan's premier, why Taiwan still had martial law, he had to answer that Taiwan really didn't have martial law because there was no curfew and no troops were in the streets. Chiang more than once asked Wang to read him the emergency decree (chieh-yen ling) and explain whether, if the decree were lifted, the legal basis would still exist to reimpose it if needed. "So I think," Wang stated, "that the president's first priority was to lift the state of emergency so long as the premise could be assured that no damage would be done to national security.[11]

Wang's reminiscences accord with the account of Ma Ying-jeou, Chiang's English-language secretary during the years in question. Although Ma judged that the pressure of international public opinion was not the main factor in the reform decision, he recalled that as early as 1984 CCK asked him to gather materials on how Westerners understood Taiwan's chieh-yen.[12]

The issue of martial law was particularly galling in Taiwan's relations with its intrusive and self-righteous ally, the United States, especially after the murder of writer Henry Liu in California in 1984 by gangsters hired by Taiwan's military intelligence authorities. The Formosan Association for Public Affairs (FAPA), an organization of Taiwan-born U.S. residents and citizens, became highly effective as a political lobby after its founding in 1982, and gained several important congressional allies including senators Clairborne Pell (D-R.I.) and Edward Kennedy (D-Mass.) and representatives Jim Leach (R-Iowa) and Stephen Solarz (D-N.Y.).

Also setting the scene for CCK's reform decision was the wave of democratic transitions which started in Southern Europe and Latin America in the mid-1970s and spread to South Korea and the Philippines in the 1980s. After the fall of Marcos, the opposition in Taiwan raised the slogan, "Why is it that the Philippines can, and Taiwan can't?" However, we have not found any evidence about what CCK specifically thought of these events.

The PRC Factor

The rival regime across the Taiwan Strait presented a growing threat to Chiang's regime in several ways, and political reform can be understood partly as a response to each of them.

First, the perceived PRC threat to Taiwan's security was increased by the breaking of U.S.-ROC relations by President Jimmy Carter in 1979. As CCK told a German reporter, "President Carter has repeatedly emphasized that the establishment of U.S.-

communist bandit relations will not create any threat to our people's prosperity, security, or welfare. But if we look at Carter's public statements on the 'normalization' of relations with the Chinese communists, the U.S. has no clear arrangements for guaranteeing the security of the Taiwan area after the establishment of U.S.-bandit relations; they just proceed on the basis of the American hypothetical judgment that the bandits 'have no intention' and 'have no capability' to invade Taiwan. This kind of hypothesis is very dangerous."[13] The PRC followed up their normalization breakthrough by launching a campaign to induce Taiwan to accept peaceful unification. Beijing offered Taipei the right to keep its own political, social, and economic system under the formula of "one nation, two systems." The PRC campaign gained added force when the Reagan administration agreed to the 1982 Shanghai communique promising gradually to decrease the quantity and quality of U.S. arms supplies to Taiwan, and in 1984 when China and Britain signed an agreement on the future of Hong Kong that provided for using the one-nation-two systems formula there.

KMT political concessions to the native Taiwanese populations had long been linked with PRC pressure. As Hung-mao Tien wrote in 1975, "The party leadership has been compelled by the disheartening diplomatic events [like expulsion from the U.N. in 1971] to undertake measures for the purpose of fortifying internal solidarity and to pacify discontented Taiwanese."[14] These measures included recruiting increasing numbers of Taiwanese into the ruling party and into high positions in government, increasing the number of locally elected ("supplementary") seats in the Legislative Yuan and National Assembly, and allowing the nonparty opposition (Tang-wai, or TW) more freedom to compete.

As detailed below, derecognition brought a temporary halt in the reform process that was already slowly getting under way in the late 1970s. But in a longer time perspective, CCK's subsequent decision to resume and accelerate political reform may be interpreted as an attempt to strengthen the KMT's ability to survive on Taiwan after derecognition. As CCK told a Spanish reporter in April 1979 when asked what would happen if America ceased to supply weapons to Taiwan, "A nation's defense strength does not rely on weapons. More important is to firm up our faith in and will for freedom."[15] By increasing the party's staying power in its Taiwan base, the reforms would signal that the KMT was not to be forced into negotiations with the CCP at a time not of its own choosing, that it intended to survive and prosper as long as necessary in Taiwan in order to reunify China on its own terms. Such a signal would also serve to reassure the local population that no sell-out of their interests was imminent, thus further increasing the regime's domestic security, and would disabuse the mainland authorities of any over-optimism about their prospects for easily enticing KMT-ruled Taiwan into the motherland's embrace.

Second, CCK's reforms appear to have responded not only to the PRC political-diplomatic offensive against Taiwan, but also to the threat to Taiwan's image as the freer of the two Chinas that was presented by political events in the mainland. These events included Democracy Wall (1978-79), the promulgation of a new and ostensibly more liberal PRC Constitution in 1982, the first and second rounds of direct elections of county-level people's congresses (1979-81 and 1984), the progressive liberalization of the PRC media, and Deng's licensing of discussion of political reform in 1986. Deng Xiaoping's picture appeared twice on the cover of *Time* magazine in the 1980s, and he was widely hailed in the West as leading China into an era of freedom and, some said, capitalism.[16]

On the other hand, CCK insisted that the mainland regime had not changed its spots. He told Katharine Graham of the *Washington Post*, "There are certain changes taking place. But they are cosmetic. The essence of communism remains the same."[17] He seemed to believe that the communist regime was bankrupt and making superficial concessions in order to retain its hold on power. Even so, his remarks seemed to imply that PRC democratization initiatives posed a challenge which Taiwan had to answer. For example, he stated in 1981, "Especially today when the communist bandit regime is near the end of its road, with its vile reputation known to everyone, and the communist system has been proven a total failure . . . it is more important than ever for us to strengthen the construction of constitutional government to demonstrate clearly that the strong contrast between the two sides of the Taiwan Strait is basically due to the fact that one side has implemented a constitution based on the Three People's Principles while the other has not."[18]

Third, CCK's statements indicate that not only did he not intend to negotiate a surrender to the communists, but he actually believed that the KMT would eventually recover the mainland through political means. In 1979 he told a German reporter, "The late President Chiang [Kai-shek] used to say that recovering the mainland depended on '70% political, 30% military'. . . . We are going to use our achievements in building a democratic and free society on Taiwan based on the Three Principles of the People, to exert a strong political influence on the Chinese people on the mainland. . . . So long as our actions [in recovering the mainland] receive the warm support of the mainland compatriots, they won't lead to a world war."[19] The achievement of prosperity on Taiwan under the Three People's Principles, he told a KMT party plenum the same year, "has established a good model for the future construction of a free, peaceful, strong, and unified modern China. We have established an unbeatable position in our struggle to the death with communism!"[20]

Even today, when the CCP regime in the mainland is as weak as it has ever been, such reasoning seems unrealistic to most observers. Yet it may have played a part either in Chiang's thinking about reform or at least in his ability to persuade more conservative forces in the party to accept reform. In his October 1986 interview with Graham, he stated, "Abolishing the emergency decrees is for the purpose of speeding up democratic progress here. We must serve as a beacon light for the hopes of one billion Chinese so that they will want to emulate our political system."[21]

Ma Ying-jeou recalled in an interview after Chiang's death that "He felt at the time that the domestic conditions were mature. [This was the main point.] But also, strengthening democratic politics was an important step for improving our international image and appealing to the mainland brethren. We had a saying that the mainland should emulate Taipei in politics, but what in our politics should they emulate? If our level of democratization was insufficient, did that mean we wanted them to emulate our use of martial law? President Chiang was perfectly clear about this point."[22]

Opposition Pressure and Election Timing

In explaining the need for reform, CCK often stressed the maturity of social conditions, stating that 30 years of peace and prosperity and the spread of education had raised the people's demands on the government for opportunities for political participation.[23] As we read them, these statements did not so much reflect a social-scientific analysis of preconditions for democracy as referred to the outcome of a complicated history of "transactions" (to adopt the term recommended by T. J. Cheng) between Chiang and the opposition over the course of a decade or more. Through these transactions—some public and some probably secret and still unknown—CCK and the opposition found their way to a mixed relationship of conflict and compromise that made the reforms possible. This dramatic record of conflict and cooperation included some sharp clashes, but ultimately led to the creation of sufficient common ground to enable CCK to manage his reforms successfully. That the reform did not occur either sooner or later than it did appears to have had much to do with this interaction.

The nascent opposition first entered the electoral arena in 1969 in the shape of a few non-KMT independents, when K'ang Ning-hsiang and Huang Hsin-chieh were elected respectively to the Taipei city assembly and the Legislative Yuan. In the early 1970s, CCK tried and ultimately failed fully to coopt the emerging Taiwanese political elite into the KMT.[24] People like Chang Chün-hung, Hsu Hsin-liang, and Su Nan-ch'eng got started as promising young KMT members but broke away from the party either because the rules of party life frustrated their ambitions or because they could not accept the limits the party set on their political views. Other future leaders of the opposition like K'ang Ning-hsiang and Yao Chia-wen never joined. The KMT was no longer able to absorb all the aspiring participants into its own ranks.

In 1977 the non-KMT made a breakthrough and began to take shape as a real opposition rather than as a congeries of independents. Opposition candidates won two county magistracies and two mayorships, and did well also in the polling for the Taiwan Provincial Assembly (other local posts were also elected at the same time). The KMT handled relatively mildly a riot in Chungli triggered by a dispute over the balloting. The opposition geared up strongly for December 1978 elections for National Assembly and Legislative Yuan supplementary seats. According to one observer, "It seemed as if Taiwan had reached the threshold of a multiparty system."[25]

But the December 1978 elections were canceled, the reason given being Carter's recognition of the PRC. The TW split into a moderate and a radical faction, the former committed to electoral politics, the latter to mass action. Frustrated members of the opposition tried to step up pressure on the KMT, founding *Mei-li-tao* magazine and mounting mass meetings and demonstrations. The confrontation culminated in the Kao-hsiung incident of 10 December 1979, and the jailing of eight opposition politicians for long terms.

The impetus toward gradual political change resumed a year later. The elections delayed from 1978 were carried out in December 1980 under a new election law administered by a new election commission. They were deemed reasonably fair, although the KMT did better than before.[26] Through the 1980s, the KMT made gradual concessions while the TW leaders not in jail stepped up their challenge. The TW developed the posture of a somewhat loyal opposition within somewhat stable rules of the game, campaigning hard in elections while constantly criticizing the unfair aspects of the electoral system.

In the mid-1980s, demands within the TW to organize a political party grew stronger. The opposition needed a party or party-like organization for several purposes: to gain legitimacy, to channel financing, to seek agreement on issues, to arrange for cooperation during campaigns, and most importantly, to negotiate the coordination of candidacies in order to avoid undercutting one another under the rules of Taiwan's "single vote multi member" (SVMM) electoral system. In 1980 the TW formed an electoral assistance association (hou-yuan hui). In 1985 they organized a TW Central Election Assistance Association (Tang-wai hsuan-chü chung-yang hou-yuan hui) and produced a common electoral platform, which included the demand for formation of a new party. TW-KMT relations became tense as the TW increased pressure in late 1984 and 1985.

CCK had authorized a number of informal contacts (goutong) with the opposition, first via newspaper publisher Wu San-lien in 1978. In 1985, right after the founding of the Tang-wai Research Association on Public Policy (TRAPP) and of the radical Editors' and Writers' Association (Pien-lien hui), four professors (Hu Fu and others) on their own initiative spent several months mediating to prevent the KMT from cracking down on these organizations. Not long after, the liberal senior KMT politician T'ao Pai-ch'uan came back from overseas and got CCK's blessing for another stage of "goutong."[27]

The timing and character of the 1986 reforms was crucially affected by the relationship that the two sides had arrived at through a process of mutual testing. The opposition was neither weak and disorganized like that in mainland China and many other socialist states in the late 1980s, nor was it armed and antisystem like many of those in Latin America in the 1960s. Rather, it was a relatively strong, fairly well organized, ambitious and aggressive movement which was, nonetheless, basically nonviolent, semi-loyal to the system, and willing to play within, or around the edges of, the rules of the game even as it challenged and tried to change some of them. It was an opposition that used the legal system, the electoral system, the public opinion system, even street demonstrations, but which after extended internal debate, and numerous arrests at the hands of the government, had decided to abjure systematic violence. By 1986 the opposition CCK faced was at the same time one that was putting enormous pressure on him and one that he could talk to. That he faced this sort of opposition is a key factor for explaining both how he was able to make the reforms that he did and the fact that he felt it necessary to do so.

Just as the opposition differed from oppositions in the socialist and Latin American examples, so CCK's regime differed from those models. It was neither ideologically and financially bankrupt, as were many of the socialist regimes of the late 1980s, nor was it as repressive as those regimes or as the Latin American military and corporatist regimes of the 1960s. CCK used police powers not to eliminate the opposition but to set limits to it—specifically, in an only partly successful attempt to deter it from raising the issue of Taiwan independence and from using the tactics of street violence or insurrection—and to induce it to accept his regime's rules of the game. His selective resistance to the TW and intermittent use of repression forced the TW to go through a long process of internal struggle which ultimately gave rise to its broad internal consensus to play more or less by the rules of the game. That the reforms did not occur earlier may have been partly due to the time consumed in this process of shaping a more acceptable opposition, although it is probably equally true that the long delay in reform helped to fire the determination of the opposition's more radical wing.

In any case, by 1986, CCK and the more moderate TW leaders understood one another well and were moving, with or without conscious coordination, in such a way as to outflank together both the KMT conservatives and the TW radicals.

At the time of CCK's reforms, important elections were in the offing. Scheduled for 6 December 1986, they would fill seats in the Legislative Yuan and National Assembly. By getting reform under way before these elections, CCK could seize credit for the KMT and improve its electoral performance. As James Soong stated in an interview after CCK's death, "There wouldn't be another election for three years after that, and Mr. Ching-kuo hoped that the KMT could do its preparatory work well and could do so on its own initiative, rather than being led by the nose by others. This doesn't mean that Mr. Ching-kuo hadn't been thinking about these matters earlier, but now he felt the time was becoming more and more ripe. It was necessary to break through all difficulties and to move as fast as possible."[28]

At the same time, the prospect of elections had caused the opposition virtually to make up its mind to organize a political party even before it was legal to do so, in order to provide the organizational resources it needed to perform well against stiff KMT competition (after having done relatively poorly in 1983). The decision by the exile opposition politician Hsu Hsin-liang to organize a party abroad also stimulated the in-island politicians to do so before they were outflanked from abroad.

Toward the end, Chiang and the TW got into a race to the finish line. Chiang may have hoped that he could preemptively announce the prospective legalization of the inevitable new party and thus avoid an ugly confrontation. But with CCK moving in the direction of legalization, the TW politicians for their part could not afford to wait for him, lest they be viewed as timid creatures of the ruling party. So the TW won the race; the party was established in September 1986 before Chiang had made his intentions clear, leading to a brief period of concern lest he authorize the arrest of those who had participated in the founding.

Chiang's response, however, was typical of his transactional style of dealing with the opposition. In his October 1986 interview with Graham, while stating that permission to form new parties would be announced soon, he also gave a negative evaluation of the newly established DPP, stating that the party lacked a "concept of the nation" and had failed to include the policy of anticommunism in its party charter. In effect, he was telling the DPP what conditions it would have to meet to enjoy the benefits of legalization—inviting DPP to the negotiating table and giving them the opening bid.[29] Chiang's subsequent behavior was in the same vein—declaring the DPP illegal but not arresting its members, warning against advocacy of Taiwan independence, and including in the draft civic organizations law the three conditions of anticommunism, non-advocacy of separatism, and loyalty to the constitution. All this put the burden on the DPP either to fit within the framework Chiang was establishing or to take on the risks of challenging the framework.[30]

It is often argued that opposition pressure forced CCK to reform.[31] This analysis is true as far as it goes. Had the opposition been weaker, Chiang might not have undertaken the reforms despite the existence of other factors we have identified as pushing him toward change. However, we can also say that had the opposition been substantially more aggressive than it was, the reforms might also not have been feasible, or at least might not have unfolded as smoothly as they did. Equally, had CCK been less skillful, the opposition might not have been induced to play as constructive a role as it did. Also less often noted is the way in which Chiang and the opposition mainstream helped each other in dealing both with anti-reform forces within the KMT and with more radical forces in the opposition.

The Need for Reinvigoration of the Ruling Party

Reviewing the events of the year before CCK's reform decision, James Hsiung wrote, "An eerie sense of crisis, at the start of the year [1985], hung over the open trials of the principals charged with the murder of Henry Liu, a Chinese-American writer in California [murdered in 1984]. Then came the collapse, in tandem, of the Tenth Credit Cooperative, a big-name savings and loan institution, and its sister investment outfit, Cathay Investment and Trust Co. A number of ranking government officials were implicated in the failures, which victimized numerous creditors. These, plus other mishaps... generated a momentary aura of doom...."[32]

Whether Chiang Ching-kuo shared in the sense of doom is not known, but there is some evidence that these events—as well as others that had accumulated earlier such as the murder of three relatives of TW personage Lin Yi-hsiung in 1980 and the death in policy custody in 1981 of Ch'en Wen-ch'eng, an American professor of Taiwanese origin—convinced him that the ruling party was losing its revolutionary elan and needed to renew itself. The Henry Liu incident cut especially close to Chiang because his son, Hsiao-wu, was widely accused of being the man behind the murder (an accusation that has never been proven). The Tenth Credit incident involved KMT Secretary-General Chiang Yen-shih, a close Chiang adviser, who resigned in its aftermath. Both the Ch'en Wen-ch'eng incident and the Henry Liu incident also led to increased criticism of the KMT in the United States. And both were mistakes committed by the security apparatus, which Chiang had virtually built in the 1950s.

Chiang may have felt that subjecting the ruling party to more media and electoral oversight and to increased political competition would revitalize its sense of mission, help get rid of some incompetent people, strengthen the party's image, and improve its links to the people. The party's victories over the opposition in the semi-open elections of the late 1970s and early 1980s showed that it had strong organizational roots and substantial public support. This was not a party that would collapse at the first breath of challenge but one that had the resources to rise to the challenge. As stated by K'ang Ning-hsiang, not a Chiang intimate but a close observer, "The KMT's strongman era was coming to an end. If they wanted their third generation to continue ruling Taiwan, they had immediately to adjust their relations with Taiwan society or suffer severe problems. . . . The question of foreign evaluations and the international situation was secondary. If they could get good international reviews while guaranteeing the survival of their regime, so much the better.[33]

According to Ma Ying-jeou, "I believe he was very grieved that things like this [Henry Liu and Tenth Credit] had occurred during his second term as president. That was why he decided to hold the Third Plenum. Although there was no clear declaration, the comrades inside the party knew that 'although it will not be called an overhaul (kai-tsao), it will be an overhaul in effect.'."[34] (The term kai-tsao evokes major personnel reshuffles in KMT history such as the purging of the communists in 1927 and the party reorganization in 1949 after defeat on the mainland.)

At a conference of the KMT Standing Committee on October 15, 1986, which endorsed CCK's reform policy, CCK said (using a phrase that was much quoted from then on), "The times are changing, the environment is changing, the tides are also changing. To meet these changes the ruling party must adopt new concepts and new methods and on the basis of the democratic and constitutional political order, push forward measures of reform and renewal. Only in this way can we link up with the tides of the times, only in this way can we remain forever at one with the people." In the same speech he stressed the need for the ruling party to maintain a constant attitude of self-criticism and to have the courage to make the necessary changes in itself.[35] While these phrases were typically vague and formulated, they seem to have referred to the need to revitalize the party.

The reforms suited the interests of members of the KMT's so-called "young Turk" wing (shao-chuang p'ai), people like Chao Shao-k'ang whose careers depended on winning elections rather than on bureaucratic promotions within the party machine. There is no reason to think that this group had enough clout to pressure the president. But the fact that it existed presumably made it more possible for CCK to contemplate reform, since his own party had within it the kind of personnel it would need to respond successfully in a more competitive political environment.

On the other hand, "The opposition to reforms from the right wing of Chiang's ruling party is so strong that only a leader of his standing is likely to be able to bring even the beginnings of meaningful change."[36] As we will argue in the next section, the very strength of the party's conservative faction may have been one consideration motivating Chiang to undertake the reform, knowing that if he did not do so, his weaker successors would have a hard time doing it themselves. Also, since both the Ch'en Wen-ch'eng and Henry Liu incidents involved the security-military sector, these events may have weakened the political influence of this sector or may have helped persuade CCK to decrease his reliance on them.

Health and Succession

CCK had long suffered from diabetes. He was 60 when he took the office of president in 1978 for a six-year term. In 1981 and 1982 he underwent eye surgery for retinal bleeding, and in 1985 he had cataract removal surgery. Both conditions were connected with his worsening diabetes. Also in 1985, according to *Newsweek*, he had a pacemaker implanted. Describing his appearance at Katharine Graham's October 1986 interview with him, *Newsweek* said that Chiang "moves slowly, with apparent pain, and his hands tremble."[37]

In 1983 CCK had demoted the second most powerful man in his regime, Wang Sheng, head of the military's political warfare department, to the post of ambassador to Paraguay. It is generally believed that he did so because Wang had been acting too independently and challenging the president's power. His heir apparent, the popular and able Prime Minister Sun Yun-suan, suffered a cerebral hemorrhage in 1984. Also in 1984, when accepting his second term as president, Chiang chose Lee Teng-hui as his vice president and hence constitutional successor should he die in office.

These events, especially the state of CCK's health, brought the sensitive succession problem into the realm of public debate.[38]

Although CCK's second term ran until 1990, speculation about his plans for succession was frequent in the early 1980s. He addressed these concerns for the first time in a *Time* magazine interview published in September 1985, stating that he had "never given any consideration" to the possibility that he might be succeeded by a family member and that the succession would be handled in accordance with "democracy and the rule of law."[39] Chiang gave a still more unambiguous statement of his position on Constitution Day, 25 December 1985, when he said that members of the Chiang family "could not and would not" (pu-neng ye pu-hui) run for the office of president and that military rule "could not and would not" take place either. (Although Chiang did mention in this short speech that his health was not as good as it used to be, from the context it appears that he was not expecting to die in office but meant to suggest that he would not be a candidate for a third term; although the constitution allowed only two terms, this provision was suspended under the Temporary Provisions.)[40]

There is no direct evidence as to why he took this position against family succession. It may be significant that he made his statement not long after the reputation of his second son, Hsiao-wu, was damaged by charges that he had given the order for the murder of Henry Liu. (The eldest son, Hsiao-wen, was chronically ill; the third son, Hsiao-yung, is a businessman who has never been seriously involved in politics. CCK also had a younger half-brother, Wei-kuo, whom some have regarded as a potential successor. The two had been political rivals in the past; we do not know what CCK's attitude toward Wei-kuo was in the 1980s.) The public discussion of the succession issue had revealed widespread distaste for a family succession, articulated especially strongly by the opposition press.

The succession issue may have affected Chiang's thinking on political reform in two ways. First, with his retirement or death the political system would lose a popular leader whose personal legitimacy (derived from a mix of family heritage, connections, and political skill) was important to bolster the regime. Chiang may have wished to begin the process of giving that regime greater long-term security based on its ability to win competitive elections. Since he had decided for whatever reasons that he could not be succeeded by a family member, a collective leadership of KMT oligarchs, or a military man, he may have felt that only democratic political reforms could give his civilian, non-Chiang successor, whoever he might be, a good chance to consolidate power. As a "foreign observer" told Daniel Southerland of the *Washington Post* in October 1986, "Chiang wants in his final years in office to bequeath some kind of stable, lasting system, and has concluded that the only way he can do this is to invite broader participation in the political process."[41]

Second, insofar as implementing constitutional government was his goal (as we argue below), Chiang probably realized that it would be harder for a successor to implement reforms over the opposition of conservative forces in the KMT and the military than for him to do so himself. If reforms were to have a good chance of success, he would have to initiate them, which in view of his health gave him little time to act.

We have uncovered no direct evidence on these points. But in any case Chiang acted as if reform were a matter of special urgency as his health deteriorated. During 1986, in public statements to party organs charged with reform tasks, he frequently urged rapid action.[42] James Soong recalled that after the Third Plenum Chiang "expressed himself very urgently and clearly" on the issue of reform.[43] According to Ma Ying-jeou, the day before his death CCK asked party secretary Li Huan whether the CEC meeting at which parliamentary reform would be discussed was scheduled for the next day. "The impression he gave me," Ma recalled, "was that he was in a big hurry, probably because he knew about his health situation. . . . One can say that ever since the Third Plenum, he had been hoping for reform extremely urgently."[44]

The succession problem may have affected not only CCK's calculations but those of the TW and hence the challenges with which CCK had to contend. According to one contemporary report, "TW personalities figure that the TW camp has to get a party organized while CCK is still alive; only in this way can they avoid another big wave of political arrests or even bloodshed. Otherwise, it will be hard to predict the attitudes of the authorities in that post-CCK era towards a TW political party."[45] If, as we argued earlier, the threat of an impending TW party organization was one of the forces that pressed Chiang to act, then this threat in turn may have been partly a result of the succession crisis.

CCK's Political Values and Sense of Mission

CCK's reform decision was dramatic and surprised many both abroad and in Taiwan. Yet it was not a sudden decision. Preparation for it went back a long way—to the values of "constitutional government and democracy" always espoused by the KMT; to values long voiced by CCK himself; to years of opposition demands; and to earlier CCK policies.

In his early years on Taiwan, CCK played a very tough role. He served as head of the General Political Warfare Department of the army, where he installed a Soviet-style commissar system, established the China Youth Anti-Communist National Salvation Corps to control youth, and became the head of the regime's National Security Bureau and, in Edwin A. Winckler's phrase, its "security czar." According to Tillman Durdin, "operating in the shadows, CCK became one of the most feared men in the leadership. He had no apologies for the repression that went on well into the 1970s."[46]

But either then (as he insisted) or some time later, democratization also became one of his long-term goals. From the time he became premier in 1972, if not earlier, the regime began gradually to liberalize, allowing more participation, recruiting more Taiwanese to party membership and government posts, and allowing somewhat more freedom of speech. All the same kinds of factors we adduced above for the 1986 reform decision probably played a role in this series of gradual reform measures—PRC and international pressure, the rise of the opposition, and so forth. In addition, however, his words and actions reveal an orienting set of values behind his political strategies.

In April 1975, Chiang Kai-shek died and Ching-kuo, serving as premier, became the top leader. In a speech to the National Assembly on Constitution Day, 25 December, CCK affirmed his commitment to the goals of "democracy and legal system, and full implementation of the constitution," and said, "We have already established an excellent basis for putting democratic politics into effect in the recovery base [Taiwan]. Five days ago we smoothly completed the election for supplementary Legislative Yuan members. In this election, not only did the election organs fulfill the requirements of 'fair, just, and open,' but also we could see from the candidates' excellent political comportment and the voters' enthusiasm that our citizens are full of keenness for political participation and concern for national affairs, and that they have a high level of commitment to electing virtuous and capable candidates that a democratic country's citizens should have when they exercise their citizens' rights."[47]

As we have seen in many quotations adduced earlier, Chiang constantly referred to Sun Yat-sen's Three Principles and to the long-term party program of moving from tutelage to democracy. For example, in his speech on Constitution Day (25 December) 1973, Chiang stated, "We have now implemented the constitution for half of our republic's 72-year history. In the first 36 years our nation suffered internal rebellion and external invasion, yet in the midst of blood and tears we still bravely persisted in carrying forward the steps laid down in our National Father's [Sun Yat-sen's] *Outline for Nation-Building* (Chien-kuo ta-kang), moving from military rule, through tutelage, into the stage of constitutional rule. In the second 36 years the full-scale implementation of constitutionalism was impeded by communist rebellion and the fall of the mainland, but we made a brilliant success of carrying out construction of democracy and constitutional government in the recovery base."[48]

Without mentioning CCK's name, Arthur Lerman argued in a 1977 article that Taiwan's "national elite" (the mainlanders) "felt a deep commitment to democracy"—which they understood, in Lerman's words, as "liberating the energies of the people and channeling them into public affairs; disciplining the energies of the people; [and] orderly discussion in search of a unified general will."[49]

Lerman's portrayal of the elite view of democracy fits CCK well, to judge by his public statements. For example, in 1975 CCK said, "As President Chiang Kai-shek used to say, 'The basic nature of democracy is equality and freedom, and the spirit of freedom means obeying the law and performing one's role [shou-fa shou-fen].' Thus the concept of rule by law is the core entity of democratic politics."[50] In 1976 he said, "The most important thing in politics is that the government should understand the people, and the people should trust the government."[51] In the same year he said that, thanks to the government's construction measures of the last three years, "the masses and the government have united together, our wills are concentrated, the people are stimulated to a spirit of struggle, their spirits are high."[52]

"When I go to the countryside on a visit," he told a group of American newspaper people, "it is to hear the people's opinions in order to understand deeply their difficulties and their needs. During the visit I do not make any immediate administrative decisions, but take what I have heard and seen back to my office to serve as reference material as I implement policy. These visits also serve to increase good feelings between government and people."[53]

There is no way to prove that such quasi-Confucian jargon is meaningful. But it fits well with two other leading themes in our analysis—the transaction model of relations between CCK and the opposition, in which he wants to give them space to operate but also wants to lead them into a law-abiding form of oppositional behavior; and the competition with the mainland regime in which CCK uses democratization to strengthen the competitiveness and fighting trim of his own political system against its rival. Since CCK's rhetoric seems to fit in well with his pattern of action, we had best take it into account in analyzing his motives for reform.

Findings and Theoretical Implications

The evidence we have been able to gather gives a better picture of CCK's probable motives than has been available before in one place and may contribute something to our understanding of his motives and style as a political leader. But because of data limitations our account is not definitive. As far as we could determine, all the factors we have considered seem to have influenced CCK's decision for reform to some extent. No single factor seems to have been decisive, and we have not seen any way even to try to weigh the relative importance of the different factors. Nor have we tried to evaluate the relative importance of "conditions" versus leadership decisions. Nothing we have discovered leads us to doubt that the ripeness of socioeconomic conditions was important for the reform. Nor does our analysis do anything to derogate from the importance of the TW role, despite our chosen focus on the choices made from the top down by CCK.

We selected this focus in order to contribute to the recent literature on democratic transitions in authoritarian regimes, a literature which eschews the "macro-oriented focus on objective conditions" in favor of a concentration on "political actors and their strategies."[54]

The Taiwan case confirms some of the axioms of this literature—for example, that a democratic transition is initiated to resolve a legitimacy problem, and that the regime that undertakes it gives up some measure of political control in the hope of improving its ability to survive. The transition is undertaken in order to increase the regime's ability to win allegiance from the citizens with reduced reliance on coercion.

More specifically, many of our findings conform to observations made by Alfred Stepan about what he calls "Path 4a," or "redemocratization initiated by the civilian or civilianized political leadership." Stepan's main example of this path is the case of Spain. According to him, this path has the best chance of being followed:

> (1) the more there are new socioeconomic and political demands from below or from former active supporters, (2) the more there is doubt or conflict about regime legitimacy rules (especially among those who have to enforce obedience), and (3) the more there is the chance that the power-holders will retain and ratify much of their power via competitive elections.

Stepan further points out that in this path, "the military-as-institution is still a factor of significant power. Thus the civilian leadership is most likely to persist in its democratizing initiative (and not to encounter a military reaction) if the democratic opposition tacitly collaborates with the government in creating a peaceful framework for the transition."[55]

This model fits Taiwan fairly well. One especially important area of fit is in the role of the opposition in both keeping pressure on the regime and cooperating with it. A second parallel is the existence of "doubt about regime legitimacy rules," although in Taiwan's case this doubt came not from the ruling party's loss of faith in its ideology, but in the long-standing conflict between this ideology and the authoritarian realities which the regime had always labeled as temporary.

Taiwan, however, differs from Spain in several ways. For one thing, the leader of the old regime did not have to die before the transition started; he started it himself, for reasons we have tried to investigate. Second, this fact in turn dictated that the military was a much less serious potential challenger to the reform, at least during its early phase when CCK was still alive, and even after his death so long as the ongoing reform could continue to carry the mantle of Chiang's blessing. Third, the cooperation provided to the reformist regime by the opposition came about in Taiwan through a long and difficult process of internal struggle within the opposition and between opposition and regime.

The fourth, and perhaps most important, way in which the Taiwan case differs is in the existence of the mainland factor in the Taiwan reform. Among nations that have begun democratic transitions, only South Korea and Taiwan are parts of divided nations. (East Germany might also be cited, but it is doubtful whether the "transition to democracy" literature is intended to apply to the breakdown of communist regimes.) In both cases, and in contrast to all other nations studied in the transitions literature, competition with the other regime has provided a key motive for democratizing reform. This motive has had two related components: the need to improve domestic legitimacy in order to create a political basis for a more effective defense capability; and the need to create a stronger political appeal to the nation's citizens on both sides of the dividing line.

Of course, the confrontations between North and South Korea and Taiwan and mainland China had been going on for 40 years before the phase we are identifying as democratic transition began. Thus a full analysis of how the "divided-nation" factor operates would require looking at the changing international environment and, again, at the always-important factors of domestic social, economic, and political conditions. But the point here is only that, given permissive conditions at home and abroad, the divided-nation factor enters the reformers' calculations of potential benefit and cost on the reform side of the ledger.

In the case of Taiwan this presents a double paradox. First, the opposition, many or most of whose members are motivated in part by the desire to assure that Taiwan never comes under mainland control, can thank the looming and threatening presence of the mainland for making their transactions with Chiang Ching-kuo more successful than they probably would have been otherwise—since, we have argued, this looming presence provided Chiang with one of his important motives for accommodating the opposition, however reluctantly. (Probably detailed research on the opposition's behavior during the reform process would show that they, too, were pushed toward more moderate and constructive behavior by the existence of the mainland threat, thus making them more acceptable to Chiang than they otherwise might have been.) Second, a democratization which was initiated to some extent because Taiwan was part of a larger China seems to be leading to Taiwan's increasingly well-established and irreversible *de facto* separation from that China, as the island's politics become more and more responsive to the preferences of the majority.[56]

ENDNOTES

This is a revised version of a paper presented at the Conference on Chiang Ching-kuo, University of Virginia, Charlottesville, Virginia, March 16-18, 1990. The authors would like to thank Columbia University's Taiwan Area Studies Program for financial support; Szu-chien Hsu for research assistance; Hsu Lu for comments; and Edwin A. Winckler and other members of the Conference for criticisms and suggestions.

ABBREVIATIONS

CCKHCYLC: *Chiang Tsung-t'ung Ching-kuo hsien-sheng hsien-cheng yen-lun chi* (Taipei: Kuo-min ta-hui mi-shu-ch'u, 1984).

CCKYLHP: *Chiang Tsung-t'ung Ching-kuo hsien-sheng yen-lun chu-shu hui-pien*, 15 volumes (Taipei: Li-ming wen-hua shih-yeh ku-fen you-hsien kung-ssu, 1981-1989).

CYJP: *Chung-yang jih-pao.*

HHW: *Hsin Hsin-wen.*

1. The characterization of the regime as soft authoritarian as of the mid-1980s is borrowed from Edwin A. Winckler, "Institutionalization and Participation on Taiwan: From Hard to Soft Authoritarianism?" *The China Quarterly* 99 (September 1984), pp. 481-499, although Winckler's argument is that the regime was just beginning to enter soft authoritarianism at the time he was writing. He characterizes the regime as still soft-authoritarian in "Taiwan Politics in the 1990s," in Harvey Feldman, Michael Y. M. Kau, and Ilpyong J. Kim, eds., *Taiwan in a Time of Transition* (New York: Paragon House, 1988), p. 234.

2. E.g., the essays by Whitehead, Przeworski, Stepan, and Cardoso in Guillermo O'Donnell, Philippe C. Schmitter, and Laurence Whitehead, eds., *Transitions from Authoritarian Rule: Comparative Perspectives* (Baltimore: The Johns Hopkins University Press, 1986).

3. Interview with James Soong, HHW, 2-8 January 1989, p. 17; also see interview with Ma Ying-jeou, HHW 89.1.2-8, p. 27.

4. Yangsun Chou and Andrew J. Nathan, "Democratizing Transition in Taiwan," *Asian Survey* 27:3 (March 1987), pp. 277-299.

5. Taiwan academic, party, and legal circles had been involved for years in public discussions of some of the key issues pertinent to the future reform, including the legal status of the martial law decree and of the various martial law provisions adopted under it, ways of reforming the representative structures prior to retaking the mainland, and how to legalize the formation of new parties. It is plausible that these debates influenced CCK, but we have not been able to locate evidence of this influence. At a minimum it seems probable that when he made the decision to adopt reform policies, this discussion had prepared a broad consensus as to what the reform would have to minimally involve.

6. Tun-jen Cheng, "Taiwan in Democratic Transition," in James W. Morley, ed., *Economic Growth and Political Change: The Experience of Nine Countries in the Asia-Pacific Region*, manuscript, p. 25.

7. Julia Leung and Barry Wain, "Chatty Chiang sheds No Light on Motives Behind His Push for Democratic Reform," *Asian Wall Street Journal*, 2 November 1987, p. 16.

8. Interview with Ma Ying-jeou, HHW, 2-8 January 1989, pp. 28-29.

9. Tillman Durdin, "Chiang Ching-kuo and Taiwan: A Profile," *Orbis* 18:4 (Winter 1975), p. 1024.

10. "President Chiang Ching-kuo's Interview with an Editor of *Der Spiegel*, May 16, 1983," *Parliament Monthly* 14:6 (June 1983), PP. 3-4.

11. Interview with Wang Chia-hua, HHW, 2-8 January 1989, p. 21.

12. HHW 89.1.2-8, p. 28.

13. CCKYLHP 12:423.

14. Hung-mao Tien, "Taiwan in Transition: Prospects for Socio-Political Change," *China Quarterly* 64 (December 1975), p. 617.

15. CCKYLHP 12:438.

16. On Deng's image in the West, see Andrew J. Nathan, *China's Crisis* (New York: Columbia University Press, 1990), Ch. 4.

17. Daniel Southerland, "Taiwan President to Propose End to Island's Martial Law," *Washington Post*, 7 October 1986, p. A18.

18. CCKHCYLC, p. 19.

19. CCKYLHP, 12:434.

20. CCKHCYLC, p. 84.

21. *Chung-yang jih-pao* 1986.10.13.1; English version in *Newsweek*, 20 October 1986, p. 31.

22. Ma interview, HHW, 2-8 January 1989, p. 28.

23. E.g., CCKYLHP 15:419-420.

24. The story through the 1983 election is recounted by Winckler, "Institutionalization and Participation," pp. 494-499. We have also drawn upon Li Hsiao-feng, *T'ai-wan min-chu yun-tung ssu-shih nien* (Taipei: Tzu-li wan-pao, 1987), and John F. Copper with George P. Chen, *Taiwan's Elections: Political Development and Democratization in the Republic of China*, Occasional Papers/Reprints Series in Contemporary Asian Studies, No. 5-1984 (64) (Baltimore: University of Maryland School of Law).

25. Jürgen Domes, "Political Differentiation in Taiwan: Group Formation within the Ruling Party and the Opposition Circles 1979-1980," Asian Survey 21:10 (October 1981), p. 1012.

26. John F. Copper, "Taiwan's Recent Election: Progress Toward a Democratic System," *Asian Survey* 21:10 (October 1981), PP. 1029-1039.

27. Li Hsiao-feng, *T'ai-wan min-chu yun-tung*, pp. 1029-1039.

28. Soong interview, HHW 89.1.2-8, p. 17.

29. *Chung-yang jih-pao* 9 October 1986, p. 2; English version in *Newsweek*, 20 October 1986, p. 31. Our thanks to Hsu Szu-chien for suggesting this analysis of Chiang's statement.

30. Analyzed in Chou and Nathan.

31. For example, Tun-jen Cheng, "Democratizing the Quasi-Leninist Regime in Taiwan," *World Politics* 61:4 (July 1989), pp. 471-499.

32. James C. Hsiung, "Taiwan in 1985: Scandals and Setbacks," *Asian Survey* 26:1 (January 1986), p. 93.

33. Tobari Haruo (Hu-chang Tung-fu), *Chiang Ching-kuo ti kai-ke* (Hong Kong: Kuang-chiao ching ch'u-pan she, 1988), pp. 77, 79.

34. Ma Ying-jeou interview, HHW, 2-8 January 1989, pp. 28-29.

35. *Chung-yang jih-pao*, 16 October 1986, p. 1. The significance of this meeting is explained in Chou and Nathan, p. 289.

36. Daniel Southerland, "Chiang Envisions Change for Taiwan," *Washington Post*, 13 October 1986, p. A18.

37. Ch'en P'ei-k'un, "T'ai-wan ti chieh-pan wei-chi," *Kuang-chiao ching* No. 157, 16 October 1985, p. 56; *Newsweek*, International Edition, 20 October 1986, pp. 28-29.

38. Ch'en P'ei-k'un, "T'ai-wan ti chieh-pan wei-chi," *Kuang-chiao ching*, No. 157, 16 October 1985, p. 56; Parris Chang, "Taiwan in 1982: Diplomatic Setback Abroad and Demands for Reforms at Home," *Asian Survey* 23:1 (January 1983), p. 42.

39. *Time*, 16 September 1985, p. 46. That this was Chiang's first comment on this issue is stated by Ch'en P'ei-k'un, "Taiwan ti chieh-pan wei-chi," *Kuang-chiao ching*, No. 157, 16 October 1985, p. 54.

40. CYJP, 26 December 1985, p. 1.

41. Daniel Southerland, "Taiwan President to Propose End to Island's Martial Law," *Washington Post*, 8 October 1986, p. A18.

42. E.g., at a meeting of the Central Standing Committee on 15 October, reported in CYJP, 16 October 1986, p. 1; and in a charge to the KMT members in the Executive Yuan involved in drafting certain reform bills, reported in CYJP, 30 October 1986, p. 1.

43. Soong interview in HHW, 2-8 January 1989, p. 17.

44. Interview with Ma Ying-jeou, HHW, 2-8 January 1989, p. 28.

45. Li Yi-an, "Taiwan ti yue-yang ta t'iao-chan," *Kuang-chiao ching* No. 165 (16 June 1986), p. 56.

46. Edwin A. Winckler, "Elite Political Struggle 1945-1985," in Winckler and Susan Greenhalgh, eds., *Contending Approaches to the Political Economy of Taiwan* (Armonk: M. E. Sharpe, 1988), p. 157; Durdin, "Chiang and Taiwan," p. 1032.

47. CCKYLHP 10:53.

48. CCKHCYLC, p. 30.

49. Arthur J. Lerman, "National Elite and Local Politician in Taiwan," *American Political Science Review* 71:4 (December 1977), pp. 1408-1409. For the broader Chinese tradition of democracy into which this view fits, see Andrew J. Nathan, *Chinese Democracy* (Berkeley: University of California Press, 1986).

50. CCKYLHP 10:53.

51. CCKYLHP 10:537.

52. CCKYLHP 10:544.

53. CCKYLHP 10:537.

54. Przeworski in O'Donnell, et al., eds., *Transitions*, p. 47.

55. Stepan, "Paths Toward Redemocratization: Theoretical and Comparative Considerations," in O'Donnell et al., eds., *Transitions*, pp. 73-75.

56. As Andrew J. Nathan has argued in "The Effect of Taiwan's Political Reform on Mainland-Taiwan Relations," in *China's Crisis* (New York: Columbia University Press, 1990), Ch. 9.

CHAPTER THREE

The Taiwan Economy In the Seventies

John C. H. Fei

(In 1972, he became President of the Executive Yuan (Premier) . . . Mr. Chiang assumed the premiership at a critical moment in the Republic of China's history. The country had just lost its seat in the United Nations, and international appeasement toward the Chinese Communists was growing . . . During his tenure as Premier, Mr. Chiang's fundamental policy was to "seek progress with stability and assure stability with progress (*wen-ting-chung ch'iu fa-chan*)." Under his leadership the government undertook the Ten Major Construction Projects (*shih-ta chien-she*) a daring move in view of the sluggish world economy at that time, the limited domestic financial resources, and the criticism that the projects were over-ambitious. But the success of the project ultimately served to stimulate other undertakings, provided a large number of employment opportunities, and mitigated the severity of the 1973-74 slump. Economic growth was maintained and the world praised the Republic of China's "Economic Miracle."*

The late President, Mr. Chiang Ching-Kuo, assumed the premiership in the seventies and had to provide leadership in the

---

**From brochure published by Government Information Office.*

formation of social, political, and economic policies at a critical moment in the history of the Republic of China. It is the purpose of this chapter to analyze the performance of the Taiwan economy under his leadership during the seventies. For this purpose it is important to know the economic background of the ten-year period (1970-1980) from a historical perspective; the late President was both a "hero created of the background of the time" (*shih-shih so-tsao chih ying-hsiung*) and a "hero that contributed much to the shaping of the events that took place in this period" (*tsao-shih-shih chih ying-hsiung*) leading to the "economic miracles" mentioned in the brochure quoted above.

This chapter will be divided into three sections. As a point of departure, we shall describe the economic background of the seventies from both a long- and short-run historical perspective. This involves the development of the idea of the transition growth of the contemporary less-developed countries in general and the ROC in particular, in the direction of economic and political modernization. For the late President will always be remembered as a statesman who provided the leadership to complete a movement toward the modernization of China, an ancient "agrarian empire." This movement has been a continual process since the land-space of China was penetrated, after the Opium War in the 19th century, by the forces of "modernization" that originated from the West in both the political sense of "democracy" and the economic sense of a society based on "science and technology" (*te-hsien-sheng, sai-hsien-sheng*). This chapter will emphasize the economic aspect of this modernization process.

Section I will continue with an analysis of the organizational characteristics of a modern economy. The brochure passage cited above, reflecting a popular image of the late President, tended to over-emphasize the historical significance of the Ten Major Constructions. While the social infrastructural investment was a visible, tangible, and popular accomplishment in the seventies, it could hardly be viewed as the core of the modernization process.

What is truly significant about the seventies is that, under the leadership of the late President, the ROC acquired the production characteristics of a modern economy typical of industrially advanced countries. When the attributes of a modern economy are highlighted, "seeking progress with stability" is far more important than the Ten Major Constructions as an achievement of the late President, for it took a statesman with both courage and wisdom to adopt a policy of stability that was farsighted (i.e., based on a keen intuitive understanding of what is inevitable in an evolutionary perspective) but unpopular in the milieu of the political-economic culture of the seventies. It takes the instinct of a politician (*cheng-k'o*) to carry out "popular projects" (e.g., the Ten Constructions), but it always takes statesmanship to uphold a policy that is somewhat unpopular.

Section II will deal with the transformation of the economy of ROC in the direction of modernization, which is expected to be completed in the last 20 years of this century. A major attribute of a modern economic system, illustrated quite well and decisively by the strength of the Japanese economy during the postwar period (especially after 1970), is the flexibility of the production structure resting on the foundation of a continual exploration of the frontier of science and technology. From the economic organization viewpoint, what lies at the heart of this flexibility is a liberalized economic system under which the time and energies of a significant number (if not the vast majority) of the total population can be directed to economic creativity—as regulated by the impartial competitive market forces relatively free from government interference.

A modern economic system requires liberalization (*tzu-yu-hua*), i.e., depoliticization of its mode of operation signified by the gradual atrophy of the political forces interfering with the operation of the markets. While "liberalization" (*tzu-yu-hua*) and "internationalization" (*kuo-chi k'ai-fang-hua*) were sloganized in the eighties in the ROC, the movement in these directions was already evident in the seventies, a time of a partial liberalization. The assessment of the historical significance of the seventies from this point of view can be accomplished by an examination of some of the major economic policies of that decade in a evolutionary perspective. This examination will be undertaken in Section III.

SECTION I

Economic Significance of the Seventies (1970-1980)

This decade was historically significant from a worldwide perspective as well as from the perspective of the modernization of less-developed countries (LDCs) that include ROC as a (particularly successful) special case. In these perspectives, the seventies were a period of growth slowdown in the outside world as the ROC pursued its externally oriented development strategy. The historical significance of the seventies and the statesmanship of the late President can be assessed only in light of these background factors, for the political economic culture at the time favored political patronage and government economic interference in a partially liberalized economy. A "stabilization policy," which accounted for much of the economic success of the ROC, was far from being a popular policy in the seventies.

Transition Growth Perspective

From a long-run perspective, for the contemporary LDCs (including Taiwan), the 40-year period (1950-1990) after the Second World War has been a period of transition growth from their prewar heritage of agrarian colonialism toward what was referred to by Professor Simon Kuznets as the epoch of modern economic growth (EMG). It is well known that of the more than 100 LDCs in the world, those in the geographic region surrounding mainland China (i.e., Taiwan, South Korea, Hong Kong, and Singapore) have been most successful. The "four dragons of East Asia" are the first group of the contemporary LDCs that will be joining the camp of the industrially advanced countries, at the latest by the end of this century.

What was referred to above as the epoch of modern growth (EMG) featured a new way of economic life ushered in by the Industrial Revolution in England during the last quarter of the 18th century. In his monumental volume (*Modern Economic Growth: Rate, Structure and Spread*) that won a Nobel Prize, Professor

Kuznets made it clear that the primary growth-promotion force in the modern epoch was the systematic exploration of the frontier of science and technology and their applications as an essential part of the art of production.

The subtitle of the book mentioned above provides us with a preliminary definition of a modern economy. What is meant by "spread" is that this modern way of life has proven to be so irresistible that once started in England, it spread to other parts of the world in the last 200 years. What is meant by "structure" (or "structure change") is the continued shift of the economic center of gravity from agricultural to nonagricultural production. What is meant by "rate" is the high speed that characterized the growth of national income and capital stock in modern technological societies.

In such a long historical perspective, the postwar economic development of the four dragons (1950-1990) was only following the footsteps of the industrially advanced countries that went through their own transition process during the 19th century. Taiwan acquired all the properties of EMG—"structural change" and "growth with high speed"—during this period. Furthermore, the fact that Taiwan is generally recognized to have entered in a new technology-sensitive stage of development (*k'o-chi tao-hsiang fa-chan chieh-tuan*) after 1980 indicates that it is quickly becoming a modern society based on science and technology, following the footsteps of Japan as a major economic power in the Pacific Basin.

The economic miracles of the four dragons occurred in a geographic region (surrounding mainland China) that is quite deficient in natural resources. The success of Hong Kong, for example, was often described as a "miracle on a piece of barren rock." When we realize that technological capability is a necessary and sufficient condition of modern economic growth, the miracle of the four dragons can be readily explained: the superiority of their human resources (i.e., their workers and entrepreneurs, with a cultural heritage that emphasized both education and a commercialism based on the institution of private property) has fully compensated for the deficiency in natural resources.

It is only natural for this region that is deficient in natural resources to adopt an externally oriented development strategy by selling labor- and/or technology-intensive manufactured goods to the world market in exchange for the "needed" imports that are natural resources-intensive. Such a natural externally oriented development strategy was, in fact, adopted in all four dragons and has accounted for their extremely successful transition growth performances. While the success of Taiwan was achieved by this externally oriented strategy, it is important for us to note that the ROC did *not* adopt this natural strategy immediately after the war.

In Taiwan, the postwar transition growth went through three subphases: the initial *import substitution phase (1959-1962)*, the *external orientation phase (1962-1980)*, and the phase of *external orientation based on technological sensitivity (1980-)* that is expected to be the last phase before economic maturity. With such a historical periodization we can see that the seventies were the second decade of the external orientation growth. The identification of the economic background of the seventies in this way is essential for any evaluation of the leadership of Chiang Ching-kuo from the economic standpoint.

By the seventies, Taiwan, by rejecting the import substitution strategy, had already found the correct (i.e., the natural) development strategy of external orientation. Moreover, while an important part of the story of success during the first decade of externally oriented growth (1962-1970) must be told in terms of the export of agricultural products, the commodity content of exports had already shifted decisively to manufactured goods in the seventies. Thus, the implementation of the externally oriented strategy in the second decade was both simpler and easier as it was resting firmly on the foundation of success in the first decade.

When viewed in this historical context, the late President was merely a "hero created by the economic background" (*shih-shih so-tsao chih ying-hsiung*) as he did not have to make an independent decision in respect to the choice of the basic national development strategy. There was already a full social consensus that the "lifeline of the economy is all out for export" (*i-ch'ieh wei-liao ch'u-k'ou*).

Worldwide Perspective

The seventies were often somewhat incorrectly characterized in the ROC. For example, it is an understatement when the quoted brochure refers to the recession of 1973-74 as a temporary "slump" that was dealt with successfully by "compensatory fiscal policies." In the past, the Taiwan public was often informed by the government that the seventies was a "decade of oil crisis." However, the experience of the seventies has proven that when an economy has acquired the technological capability to sell in the world market (by adopting an externally oriented strategy such as that of the Four Dragons or Japan), the increases in the price of crude oil will not constitute a development bottleneck factor for these oil-deficient economies.

From a historical perspective, the postwar period from 1950 to 1972 was a period of prosperity unprecedented in the 200 years since the arrival of EMG. Wave after wave of epoch-making technological innovations had brought about the "second industrial revolution" in this period. This unprecedented period of great prosperity had terminated by the early seventies, ushering in a new period of relatively slow growth which was the major characteristic of the seventies.

The reaction in the industrially advanced countries to the problem of unemployment brought about by growth slowdown was a resort to a policy of monetary expansion, calculated to lower the interest rate in order to stimulate investment. In these countries, the mainline economic policy thinking (i.e., Keynesianism) in the seventies was a blind faith in "aggregate demand management" under which the monetary authority believed that the interest rate could be lowered artificially by monetary expansions. When this policy was practiced in earnest, the result was stag-flation, a new economic term that appeared in the seventies. Instead of curing unemployment, the U.S. and European countries suffered from their unprecedented double-digit peacetime price inflation. Thus in a worldwide perspective the seventies will always be remembered as a decade of growth slowdown with price inflation, due largely to monetary mismanagement, in the industrially advanced countries.

Political-Economic Culture for Government Interference

The relevance of this "worldwide prospect" to the ROC is quite direct and obvious. As the externally oriented development strategy was in full swing, the growth slowdown in the industrially advanced countries in the seventies would adversely affect the exports of the four dragons (including Taiwan). Furthermore, as the Taiwan currency (NT) was tied to the U.S. dollar under the fixed exchange rate system of the seventies, price inflation in the outside world (i.e., the major trading partners of the ROC) was transmitted automatically into the Taiwan economy.

Thus as Taiwan entered into the second decade of external growth (1970-1980), Chiang Ching-kuo, the new premier, had to deal with a set of problems not encountered in the first decade (1962-1970), characterized by worldwide prosperity. The ROC government, like the monetary authorities in the industrially advanced countries, was under heavy pressure to "help" the domestic exporters by taking political actions. While the industrially advanced countries had blind faith in "aggregate demand management," the social consensus in Taipei in the seventies was not much more clear-minded. There was the general view that government had the responsibility to take care of the interests of its citizens (*chao-ku she-hui ta-chung chih li-i*) under a misguided interpretation of the "Livelihood-doctrine" (*san-min chu-i chung chih min-sheng chu-i*) of Dr. Sun Yat Sen.

In the early postwar years, Taiwan was not alone in harboring a blind faith in government interference. The vast majority of the contemporary LDCs began the transition growth process with a misguided internally oriented development strategy of "import substitution"—characterized by dedication to a political economy with a "socialistic tinge" that encouraged political penetration of the economic system, by public ownership (*kuo-ying shih-yeh*) or by the exercise of macroeconomic policies (e.g., the import duties, the interest and foreign exchange rates) in the name of growth promotion. This strategy was calculated with an autarchic (i.e., "internal") orientation to exclude foreign products and foreign factories (and, to a certain extent, the "foreigners") from domestic markets. Taiwan was no exception; its adoption of the highly politicized import substitution strategy to initiate the postwar transition growth (1950-1962) was believed to be consistent with the doctrine of "people's livelihood."

John C. H. Fei

The adoption of the externally oriented strategy in the ROC in 1962 amounted to a partial rejection of autarchy and the extensive government interference inherent in the import substitution strategy. However, since the Taiwan economy had had only a relatively short history (i.e., for ten years, 1962-1972) of externally oriented growth, the society was not yet quite shaken loose from the idea of government patronage under political paternalism. The sloganized demand for liberalization (*tzu-yu-hua*) and internationalization (*kuo-chi k'ai-fang-hua*) that amounted to a full rejection of government interference was a "revolution in the culture of political economy" that occurred much later, in the eighties.

To Seek Progress with Stability (wen-ting-chung ch'iu fa-chan)

Thus the seventies were an unusual period in the transition growth process of Taiwan. When the externally oriented strategy was running into difficulties because of growth slowdown in the outside world, there was a social consensus that it was the responsibility of the government to "create prosperity." Indeed, throughout the seventies (and even, to a lesser extent, at the present time), the government never hesitated to use such expressions as "to improve the investment environment" (*kai-shan t'ou-tzu huan-ching*) to suggest political activism in the economic domain. Persistent social pressures were applied to the government—e.g., through newspaper editorials—to intervene to promote exports quickly, i.e., to help the manufacturers of the exported products to make money.

These pressures boiled down to a demand for the government to manipulate three rates: the *interest rate*, the *money growth rate*, and the *foreign exchange rate* (i.e., to print more money) to lower the interest rate, and to devalue Taiwan N in official exchange rates so as to make the export products from Taiwan cheaper in the world market and the imported products more expensive, to protect the domestic market from foreign penetration). While common sense would suggest that these political interventions could hardly be expected to provide any real solution to the problem caused by recession, the mainline thinking in Taipei in the seventies was that this "convenient and costless medicine" should be prescribed.

It was only in the context of such a time—i.e., an externally originated growth slowdown *and* an internally originated demand for government intervention—that we can appreciate the meaning of "seeking progress with stability." In this regard stability can be equated with price stability, for the exercise of the three rates in the directions popularly demanded will cause price inflation sooner or later, if carried out earnestly. It took the courage and wisdom of a statesman with a sufficiently high political stature to uphold a policy of stability that was socially quite unpopular in the seventies. It was in this sense that the late president was a "hero that created the time" (*tsao-shih-shih chih ying-hsiung*).

My conjecture is that when Chiang Ching-kuo took over the premiership in the seventies he was still haunted by the bitter memory of price inflation that had contributed to the loss of the mainland to the Communists. He probably also had the intuitive understanding that expeditious political actions calculated to benefit a small social group (i.e., the exporters who were the dominant vested interest group in the seventies) cannot be socially costless (i.e., cannot avoid inflicting a loss on other social groups victimized by price inflation). The fundamental policy of "seeking progress with stability" was adhered to and, consequently, Taiwan was able to maintain a steady pace of rapid growth with relative price stability in the seventies, a period of difficulties from both the political and economic standpoint.

SECTION II

Modernization of Taiwan

The seventies were a period that wrote the final chapter in preparation for both the political and economic modernization of China. In an evolutionary perspective, a transformation in the direction of modernization implies a rearrangement of government-society relations in such a way as to curb the arbitrariness in the exercise of governmental power that is inconsistent with explicitly expressed social preferences and choices.

John C. H. Fei

A modern institution implies, intrinsically, a distrust of the political power—especially when a channel of government-society dialogue is not institutionalized. To insist on the atrophy of the political force as a prerequisite for modernization is particularly important and relevant in the twentieth century. After witnessing the failure in the experiment in communism in the last 70 years (1920-1990) or the bankruptcy of "socialistic experiments" [e.g., the "welfare statism" in the United States or the "curbing of private enterprises" (*chieh-chih ssu-jen tzu-pen*) under the "People's livelihood doctrine" (*min-sheng chu-i*) in the ROC] in the last 30 years (1950-1980), we can say categorically that the twentieth century is quite unusual in the extent and the severity of arbitrary interference by political forces in private economic life. It is not an accident that the call for liberation from government interference is a common voice in the last 20 years of the twentieth century.

While the "atrophy of political force" is a negative characterization of a modern institution at the present time, there are positive reasons for this insistence. Ultimately, a modern polity (i.e., a political institution) promises constitutional democracy, while a modern economic system promises competitive markets. These institutions, which uphold the cultural values of "freedom of choice" and "self-reliance," are modern because they are conducive to social progress that can be realized only through fuller exploration of the "inner content of human being" (*p'ei-yang jen-hsing chih nei-han*) and continued cultivation of a social norm of distributional justice. Modern institutions ensure an evolutionary unfolding of a new and a better world (*shang-jih-hsin, jih-jih-hsin, yu-jih-hsin*) in an experimental process that involves persuasion and compromise.

In the case of Taiwan, the eighties will always be remembered as a period of rapid transition toward constitutional democracy in which the late president played a catalytic role before his death in 1988. What was true for political modernization was paralleled by the economic modernization, the meaning of which will now be explored.

Flexibility of a Modern Economic System

In addition to the properties of modern economic growth emphasized by Professor Kuznets—i.e., rapid capital accumulation and rapid change of the "dualistic structure" of the economy (see last section)—we can add a third property, namely, the *flexibility of the production structure* or a healthy metabolism characterized by the timely birth of new products in new industries and the timely death of old industries as they become obsolete. A modern economic system is comparable to a biological entity in which metabolism, a sign of health and vitality, is the natural consequence when the economy has mastered the art of the exploration of the frontier of science and technology. The material well-being will be enhanced as the society constantly renews its vitality.

Material well-being, however, is only a part of the story. For under the competitive market system, a modern economy provides opportunities for all to explore the virtually unlimited potential of technology by the equally unlimited "inner potential" of human beings. The distributional justice of such an economy is based on dedication to the cardinal principal of *rational egalitarianism*, i.e., reward according to meritorious performance with equal opportunity for participation. Under rational egalitarianism, a significant portion of the total population can be motivated by self-interest to devote their time, energy, and talent to creative activities (e.g., to be scientists, engineers, entrepreneurs, professors, lawyers, or accountants) that will be socially beneficial in bringing about *progress* in the direction of a new and better world.

A quick glance at an old "Sears Catalogue" will convince the readers how rapidly the commodities which we consume daily can change, in price and in quality, in the short span of 20-30 years. (A mechanical desk calculator that cost $700 in the late fifties is now replaced by a $3 pocket-size computer with infinitely higher calculating capacity.) This technological flexibility has contributed to the "miracle on the rock" of Hong Kong, the colossal economic empire of Japan, and the success of the externally oriented drive of the Taiwan farmers who, with their meager natural resources, can produce wave after wave of new products (mushroom, pineapple, banana, pork, fruits, shrimps) for the world market.

In all these cases the flexibility of the production structure is the result, and can only be the result, of an economic creativity motivated by rational egalitarianism and regulated by competitive market forces. For those who are not professional economists, competition can imply something aggressive and antisocial, as it is often equated with cut-throat activity that favors the strong and discriminates against the weak. In fact, competition implies a dedication to accomplishment as well as rivalry with impartiality and fairness.

Flexibility of the Competitive Market

While structural flexibility is the *sine qua non* for a modern economic system, the institutional arrangement that brings about this property is the competitive market system, for technically a competitive market system is only an information system, i.e., an arrangement whereby all market participants are price (information) takers who can engage in transactions at the same market prices without discrimination. One can go one step further by describing a competitive system as an idealized arrangement under which all participants are oblivious of the very existence of competitors as, indeed, all individual choices for production and consumption are guided only by information on the relative value of goods and services. A competitive system implies impersonal rivalry with impartiality.

It is such a competitive market system that has contributed to the structural flexibility and healthy metabolism of the capitalistic economy that has evolved, mainly in the nineteenth century. The evolution toward such a system was the most important achievement of the Taiwan economy in the externally oriented growth process (1962-1980). The economic miracle of the four dragons (including Taiwan) was primarily a story of the success of a competitive market system.

The very meaning of the renunciation of import substi-tution growth (1950-1962) and redirection of the development strategy toward external orientation (1962-1980) was dedication to the competitive market. This is due primarily to the fact that the penetration of the economic system by political forces—characteristic of an import substitution process—cannot extend beyond the territory of a sovereign state. The exports of the four dragons must compete in price and quality in a foreign land (e.g., the U.S. market) that does not recognize the label of "national origin." It was mainly through competitive discipline in the foreign market (1962-1980) that the Taiwan producers acquired the fine art of surviving—i.e., the ability to be flexible in structural adjustment—through self-reliance.

A Period of Transformation of Economic Culture (1970-1980)

For the ROC, the seventies were a period of preparation for economic modernization primarily because it was through a learning by doing process that a social consensus was gradually formed to the effect that the guiding principle of the economy must be devotion to *liberalization* and *internationalization*—sloganized after 1980.

One should realize that these slogans really represent evolution in political-economic-cultural values in the direction of modernization. For the meaning of internationalization is to subject domestic production to the rigor of international competition not only in the foreign but also in the domestic market. It was because of such a value that the protective wall against imports and restrictions of foreign investment in Taiwan began to crumble after 1980. The slogan of liberalization called for renunciation of the exercise of arbitrary growth promotion policies—such as the three rates mentioned in the last section—that interfered with the operation of a fairly competitive system.

The seventies were thus a transition period. For although the externally oriented strategy—i.e., to be competitive in the international market—was accepted, the economy had not yet discovered the value of internationalization (i.e., to be internationally competitive in the domestic market) or liberalization (i.e., to renounce the political patronage via the exercise of economic policies). The seventies produced a mixture of liberalization and control with gradual atrophy of the latter. During this period of transition from a controlled economy to a fully modernized economy characterized by structural flexibility, the partially liberalized economy gradually gained confidence to adopt the full measures of liberalization in the eighties.

SECTION III

Policy Evolution in the Seventies

The above analysis of the seventies from a transition growth perspective can be substantiated from an examination of the evolution of the economic policies that affected the mode of operation of the economic system in this period. There are altogether five major categories of macroeconomic policies in the less developed countries to promote growth:

i) Domestic Fiscal Policies
ii) External Fiscal Policies
iii) Money and Interest Policies
iv) Foreign Exchange Policies
v) Policies on International Investments

In addition to these major policy areas there are also five auxiliary policy areas:

vi) Government Enterprises and Social Infrastructural Investment
vii) Agriculture
viii) Manpower Labor Education and Family Planning
ix) Science and Technology
x) Economic Development Planning

In this section we shall examine these policies to support the thesis that the seventies were a period of preparation for the transition into modernization accomplished after 1980. The major macro-policies involve government manipulation of three rates (see last section) to help domestic entrepreneurs and/or government shielding of domestic entrepreneurs from international competition in the domestic market. These macro-policies are intrinsically much more complex (from a technical standpoint) than the auxiliary policies because money is involved. For this reason, the auxiliary policies will be examined first.

Basically, the idea of transition into modernization attributes the economic success of Taiwan almost exclusively to the perfection of the market economy accompanied by the atrophy of the centralism of government command. As a result of this transition, the economic institutions of Taiwan gradually approximate those that are characteristic of the camp of industrially advanced countries which Taiwan will join as a full-fledged member by the end of this century. [To avoid the appearance of oversimplification, readers are referred to an alternative interpretation of the policy evolution by K.T. Li (see reference) for a more sympathetic account of political interference.]

Auxiliary Policy Areas

As a point of departure, let us consider (vi) government enterprises and social-infrastructure investment—which included the much heralded "Ten Major Construction Projects" of 1973 in the area of social-infrastructure investment. However, from a historical perspective, what is far more significant is that a social consensus gradually emerged in the seventies to the effect that the government should abandon public enterprises. A guiding economic principle of the founding Father of the republic (*min-sheng chu-i*) on the curbing of private enterprises and the upholding of public enterprises (*fa-chan kuo-chia tzu-pen*) was quietly dropped in the seventies, ending with a summary repudiation of public enterprises (*ch'ing-suan kuo-ying shih-yeh*) in 1981).

The late President was a great statesman because of his *pragmatic orientation*, i.e., his firm grasp of the idea that an economy based on political command does not work for a modern society. At the present time, as the Communist leaders on the mainland are attempting to carry out a program of total economic reform that rejects the doctrinaire position of the centralism of command of public enterprises, they have much to learn from the experience of failure in Taiwan.

In respect to agricultural policies (vii) the late President was always regarded as a political leader who was "good to the farmers" because a program that guaranteed the price of rice was adopted in 1974. However, the initiation of a price support program that benefitted the farmer was hardly the result of the personal preference of a political leader. In fact a major difference between the DC (industrially advanced) and LDC (less developed) countries is that the agricultural sector is subsidized in the former while always exploited in the latter. Thus the seventies was a period of transition growth in that the economic center of gravity shifted to the industrial sector of the economy and the ROC was beginning to adopt protective agricultural policies typical of industrially advanced countries. Regarding policies on manpower and education (viii) and science and technology (ix), we shall only remark that the seventies were a transition period. The external orientation of the sixties (1962-1970) was based on labor-intensive manufactured exports for which the comparative advantage of Taiwan was the abundance of inexpensive unskilled labor. In contrast, the external orientation after 1980 shifted to a "technological foundation" where the comparative advantage of exports became a labor force of high quality and human ingenuity—a sense conveyed aptly by a popular "Japanese image." The two policy areas (viii and ix) took on historical importance from this change in the comparative advantages of exports in the seventies.

In respect to economic planning (x), readers of the present generation must be made aware that in the postwar period up to the eighties many contemporary LDCs (including Taiwan) in the capitalistic camp operated with an economic planning commission that is conspicuous only by its absence in the industrially advanced countries. This latter group of countries (i.e., the DCs) are mature enough to know that, for a modern economy characterized by a rapid metabolism, it is beyond the capability of government bureaucrats to blueprint the operation of the whole economy by central planning.

In the seventies Taiwan did have a "Sixth Four-Year Plan" (1973-1976) and a "Six-Year Plan" (1976-1981). However, through a sequence of reforms in 1973 and 1976, the planning commission was reorganized and was converted from an agency that "plans for total resources mobilization" to one that undertakes more modest "planning for economic policy coordination"—comparable to the Council of Economic Advisers to the presidents in the United States. The period from 1970 to 1980 was a transition toward a modern economic system that rejected resource allocation by explicit bureaucratic calculations (see below).

Seeking Progress With Stability

We turn now to the major policy areas. We mentioned earlier that a guiding principle of policy formation under the premiership of Chiang Ching-kuo was stabilization (i.e., seeking progress with stability) that, given the background of a worldwide growth slowdown during an externally oriented drive, amounted to a government determination to resist social pressure for monetary expansion and price inflation. This stabilization strategy will now be examined more carefully.

In the context of the economic development of contemporary less-developed countries, sustained price inflation is essentially a politicized monetary phenomenon as purchasing power is printed by the government to finance a budget deficit and/or to finance private investment (i.e., by making purchasing power available to private investors at an artificially lowered interest rate to augment their windfall profit by political patronage). Let us examine these two causes of monetary expansion as they operated in the seventies in the ROC.

In respect to public finance, one truly important lesson that the other less-developed countries can learn from the ROC is to keep the government budget in balance (or even to run a government budget surplus) so that a government budget deficit would never be a factor contributing to price inflation. While the Taiwan government did have a budget deficit in the import-substitution era, it was the effort that brought the deficit under control in 1961 that prepared the background for the strategy of externally oriented growth in 1962. In fact a budget surplus, realized in 1964, became a tradition of "conservatism" in public finance of the ROC all through the seventies.

Taiwan has firmly rejected the policy of inflationary finance and opted for a philosophy of taxation *with* (rather than without) social consent. The ROC government never evaded the politically onerous task of seeking a consensus on tax reform, which was carried out through the setting up of a Tax-reform Commission in 1969. Throughout the seventies under the premiership of Chiang Ching-kuo, government budget deficits never appeared as a problem. In fact, when a small budget deficit appeared in 1982, the immediate response of the government was the introduction of a bill for value-added taxes that was implemented in 1986. The ROC government never abused political power and never exercised it arbitrarily for taxation without social consent.

Fiscal conservatism may be viewed as the heart of the stabilization policies. It is noteworthy that this policy was carried out in the absence of theoretical support in the seventies. In the industrially advanced countries (e.g., the United States) the seventies witnessed a rapid expansion of government budget deficits. Furthermore, mainline thinking, influenced by Keynesian orthodoxy, regarded these deficits as quite justifiable. Social concern with government budget deficits as an evil did not occur until after the eighties. Thus we see that the meticulous adherence to fiscal conservatism of the ROC under the leadership of the late President was clearly a wisdom ahead of its time.

As far as private investment finance is concerned, the ROC attempted to control price inflation with a high interest rate in the early fifties. This experiment was repeated in 1972–the year Chiang Ching-kuo assumed the premiership. Like conservatism in fiscal policies, controlling price inflation with a high interest rate was a novel idea, the practice of which was far ahead of its time. In the industrially advanced countries the mainline thinking in the seventies was that an expansionary money supply could lower the interest rates—an idea that apparently infested the Taiwanese public in the seventies (see section I). In the West, the idea that a high interest rate can be used as a quick and effective cure for price inflation was never an integral part of economic doctrine.

Thus we see that in the macro-policy area the stabilization policy of the seventies really amounted to what is now recognized as sound monetary and fiscal conservatism. Such a philosophy was not developed until after the eighties in the industrially advanced countries.

A Partially Liberated Economic System

We have mentioned that Taiwan was a partially liberated economy in the seventies, making preparation for a full transition toward liberalization in the eighties. To see the meaning of partial liberalization, we should mention two policies—the *custom rebate system* that started in the late fifties and the *export processing zone* that started in 1966—that constituted the heart of the externally oriented strategy. Both policies were calculated to encourage fair competition by Taiwanese producers in the world market, while simultaneously keeping the domestic market closed to international competition. The name used for this half-hearted devotion to competition was "to foster selling in the external market by (a politically created favoritism) selling in the internal market" (*i nei-hsiao p'ei-yang wai-hsiao*)—a popular slogan all through the seventies.

The export rebate system (i.e., to rebate the duties on imported raw materials that entered into the re-exported products) and the exports processing zone (that exempted all import duties into the zone) were institutionalized so that the Taiwan exporters would not be handicapped by a competitive disadvantage when selling in the world market (i.e., in comparison with a Hong Kong producer who did not have to pay any duties on imported raw materials). However, under these arrangements, Taiwanese housewives did not have the same privileges as U.S. housewives, because the political power of the Taiwan government was being invoked to force them to subsidize the domestic producers—while the same sovereign power obviously cannot exploit the housewives in New York. The policy of fostering exports implies the exploitation of domestic consumers via the arbitrary exercise of political power.

Thus we see that in the seventies the popular political-economic view was that the government should help the producers by the implementation of what may be referred to as an *income transfer strategy* that victimized one social group (namely, the domestic consumers), which was politically coerced to subsidize another social group (namely, the producers). In the seventies the Taiwanese economy was operating under a politicized economic system with government patronage and with hesitant dedication to competition and self-reliance as high economic cultural values.

Transition to Full Liberalization

Full liberalization of the Taiwan economy occurred in the eighties when a consensus was formed in favor of liberalization (*tzu-yu-hua*) and internationalization (*kuo-chi k'ai-fang-hua*). This full liberalization amounted to a demand for withdrawal of the political forces from the domestic commodity market and domestic investment market that were to be opened up for international competition. In the final analysis, the demand was for the ROC to adopt the *modern features of economic organizations*—structural flexibility and a healthy metabolism consistent with a distributional justice based on a rational egalitarianism—typical of industrially advanced countries.

It might appear that the collapse of the elaborate system of protective tariffs, the elimination of restrictions on foreign investment and the appreciation of the NT against the dollar that occurred in Taiwan in recent years came about as the result of political pressure from the United States. However, from an evolutionary perspective, the liberalization of the Taiwan economy in these ways is only the natural consequence of the externally oriented growth process of the seventies, i.e., a natural extension of the dedication to competition from the international to the domestic markets.

All through the period of externally oriented growth (1962-1980), a central feature of the partially controlled domestic market was based on a presumption that the bureaucrats in the government had the responsibility as well as the capability to select the direction of private investment. The selectivity of the "tariff wall" and "prohibition of foreign investment" as well as priority of entitlement to tax holiday under the Statute for Encouragement of Investment (*chiang-li t'ou-tzu t'iao-li*, 1960) were all based on a bureaucratic ranking of industries—an undertaking that the bureaucrats in the industrially advanced countries would never attempt. In the partially controlled economy in the seventies, such artificial ranking—usually nothing more than a rough ranking by aphorism (e.g., rising-sun, locomotive, "strategic")—was, in fact, the foundation of the income-transfer strategy though which the income of victimized social groups (the consumers and the workers) was transferred routinely to an urban entrepreneurial class that was politically favored and patronized.

The arbitrariness in the exercise of political power in the economic arena—i.e., the selection of what is "strategic" to guide an income-transfer strategy—violated the two key tenets of a modern economic system which we identified in the last section. It was unfair, and at the same time saddled the economy with structural rigidity (i.e., depriving the economy of a healthy metabolism). The unfairness of perpetual 40 percent import duties on passenger cars would certainly produce a consumer rebellion in the U.S. Congress. And yet, in Taiwan before the eighties, the fact that the domestic consumers were routinely and perpetually exploited by a much higher rate could only be the result of the immaturity of a political-economic culture that tolerated the arbitrariness of an aggressive government under a paternalistic polity.

The call for total economic reform (*she-hui chu-i; ch'uan-p'an ching-chi chih-tu kai-ko*) in socialistic countries (including mainland China) in the eighties has made it abundantly clear that centralism in economic planning (i.e., where the power to make decisions for sectoral expansion is relegated to bureaucrats) will end up with a structural rigidity (*sheng-ch'an chieh-kou chiang-hua*). The experience of Taiwan has demonstrated conclusively that "economics by political command" is not consistent with the requirement of structural flexibility of a modern technological society. (We must add that liberalization in the ROC is yet to be completed because the import duty on passenger cars is still well over 30 percent).

In summary, the seventies was a unique period in the transition of the ROC toward economic modernization. It was during the second decade of externally oriented growth that Taiwan producers gained confidence through their success in meeting the competition in the world market. It was through this learning-by-doing process that they acquired the capability to be adaptive to changes in the external environment, i.e., to be structurally flexible. But, above all, it was through such disciplines that they have acquired a cultural attitude of self-reliance, i.e., a rejection of dependence on patronage of political forces for survival.

The cultivation of the modern political-economic attitude was first accomplished by competition in the world market. However, when transition growth was viewed as a cultural phenomenon, it was only natural for the same set of values to grow and spread to economic activities that occurred internally in the domestic market. The demand for liberalization and internationalization in the eighties was thus the direct outgrowth of the success achieved in the seventies—as the ROC marches on to economic modernization and maturity.

Concluding Eulogy to the Late President

This chapter is an examination of the evaluation of the Taiwan economy in the seventies, telling a highly successful story of modernization. From a volume on the leadership of the late President, the readers have the right to learn more about his economic leadership—i.e., the extent of the responsibility for policy formation exercised by Chiang Ching-kuo, guided, inevitably, by his personal experience and economic philosophy. In this regard, we must bear in mind that a statesman is, almost by definition, one who has the wisdom and capacity to solicit sound advice from a circle of specialists—e.g., a diplomat, a military expert, or an economist—that usually excludes himself.

The economic miracle of Taiwan would not have been possible had the late President not had the intuitive insight to see through the evil and the falsehood of inflationary finance via the convenience of money printing and had he not persistently insisted on an "economic cabinet" staffed by enlightened administrators— such as minister K. T. Li, the main architect of the economic miracle of Taiwan—dedicated to a philosophy of monetary conservatism. (In this regard we must remember that all genuine economic conservatives (e.g. Friedman and Hayek) are basically "monetarists" who abhor the "politicization of money printing" that has been practiced earnestly in Latin American countries in the postwar years.)

In my last audience with him in July 1986, the late President was preoccupied mainly with the political problems related to unification with the mainland and the democratization of the polity of Taiwan—discussed in other chapters of this volume. When I expressed the view that a practical way to prepare the precondition of a political unification is the transmission to the mainland of the experience of economic success that has been achieved in Taiwan under his leadership, he responded by saying: "Please tell your fellow economists that C.K. (referring to himself by pronouncing his name in Chinese) is a layman in economics and made many mistakes during my lifetime. What I can only claim is a salvaging virtue of learning from my mistakes." He was not an economist. What is more important is that he was a human being with modesty and humility.

REFERENCES

Fei, John C. H., "Economic Development and Traditional Chinese Cultural Values," *Journal of Chinese Studies*, Vol. 3, No. 1, April 1986.

Fei, John C. H., "Sino-American Economic Relations From an Evolutionary Perspective of Taiwan's Economic Institutions," *U.S. Congressional Club Reprint Series* No. 1, Vol. 133, No. 137, September 11, 1987 Washington D.C. Values.

Fei, John & G. Ranis, *Development of Labor Surplus Economy*, Irwin Press, 1964.

King, Y. C., P. L. Lee eds., *Social Life and Development in Hongkong*, The Chinese University Press, Hong Kong.

Kuo, Shirley W. Y., Gustav Ranis and John Fei, *The Taiwan Success Story: Rapid Growth with Improved Distribution in the Republic of China, 1952-1979*, Westview Press, 1981.

Kuznets, Simon, *Modern Economic Growth: Rate, Structure and Spread*, Yale University Press, 1966.

Li, K. T., *The Evolution of Policy Behind Taiwan's Development Success*, Yale University Press, 1988.

CHAPTER FOUR

Comments on John C. H. Fei's "The Taiwan Economy in the Seventies"

Thomas A. Metzger

I first want to thank Professor Leng and his colleagues at the Miller Center for hosting this very stimulating conference. I also want to say that it is a great honor for me to comment on the work of a scholar so distinguished as Professor Fei.

The first point I would make is that I found Professor Fei's paper illuminating. His conceptualizations, of course, are typically state of the art. For instance, anyone trying to figure out the nature of the state's impact on the economy in the R.O.C. will find helpful his list of five major and five auxiliary categories of policy. I found particularly significant his account of how the government in the 1970s dealt with the global economic slowdown by emphasizing price stability rather than Keynesian remedies, and how these decisions were largely unsupported by the mainstream economic theory of the day. Similarly, Professor Fei's testimony makes still clearer to us that these wise decisions were taken in the face of much contrary thinking in KMT circles, which indeed had long been marked by an ideological inclination toward socialistic or statist, not to mention Keynesian, economic policies. Just how these decisions were made is thus an intriguing issue, as is the question of how the decision was made under President Chiang Kai-shek around 1962 to shift from import substitution to export growth. (The still earlier decision to emphasize free enterprise may have partly arisen when the KMT reacted to the 28 February 1947 Uprising.) Professor Fei has very interesting ideas about the thoughts of Premier Chiang Ching-kuo in the 1970s, his "pragmatic" grasp of economic realities, his strong memories of the inflation that helped produce the disaster of 1949. But we still want to know more about these decisions taken by him going against the grain of both KMT ideology and contemporary economics. Professor Fei himself was not exactly a stranger in Taipei then. Can it be that modesty about his own role in those affairs may be preventing him from discussing all he knows?

Professor Fei's paper, however, is not only illuminating but also provocative. Although I am not an economist, I must frankly express some doubts I feel about some of his viewpoints. I see his paper as having four main aspects: 1) his division of the R.O.C.'s economic development from 1950 on into three stages, along with his view that these stages exhibited a tendency toward decreasing governmental interference in the marketplace, and that the R.O.C.'s economic development has justly been called a "miracle"—I have no quibbles with these points; 2) his view of the causative basis for this success; 3) the policy recommendations he infers from this causative account and from theoretical considerations regarding market economies in general; and 4) the tension between his recommendations and the "people's livelihood" outlook of Dr. Sun Yat-sen.

II

With regard to the question of causes for the R.O.C.'s economic success, I am aware of four possible approaches. One approach Professor Fei mercifully does not touch on, the thesis that this success was due more to international or other situational factors than to policy and cultural patterns. While "dependency" theorists blame the economic failures of the developing world on its links with international capitalism, another school has arrived on the scene with a strangely contradictory thesis to the effect that the R.O.C.'s links with international capitalism, far from harming it, were actually the chief reason for its economic success. If this is true, however, why did the links enjoyed by the Philippines, say, fail to produce an "economic miracle"? The Philippines, after all, not only have been blessed much more than Taiwan with natural resources but also have a population largely fluent in English, the very language of so much international capitalism. To show that the R.O.C.'s economic success stemmed mainly from the economic opportunities presented to it by the international environment, therefore, one would have to show that these opportunities were better than those available to the Philippines and so many other developing countries still mired today in economic backwardness. I, at least, have never seen data showing this, and apparently Professor Fei has not either.

Scholars who say Taiwan was just lucky in enjoying exceptional international opportunities are like the Corinthian who said to Pericles: "Pericles, you're not so great. You were just lucky to be born in a great city like Athens." To which Pericles replied: "If you had been born in Athens, and I, in Corinth, then neither one of us would ever have been heard of!"

A second view, which goes back to the profound scholarship of Alexander Gerschenkron, emphasizes the contribution made by state guidance—Gerschenkron, if I understand him correctly, suggested that the more backward an economy, the larger and the more political had to be the collectivities on which the initiation of modern economic growth would depend. Therefore state guidance would be crucial for economic growth in a society as backward as Taiwan's was in 1945. Economists hostile to Milton Friedman's emphasis on free enterprise have thus harked back to Gerschenkron's perspective to explain the R.O.C.'s success, even though this Gerschenkronian view, while saving them from agreeing with Friedman, puts them in the position of praising the KMT, also a bitter pill for many of them. For many liberal or Fabian economists, having to decide whether one is more hostile to Milton Friedman or to the KMT is indeed a dilemma! Thus unable to resist making these facetious remarks, however, I in no way imply any criticism of Robert Wade's very stimulating and rigorous work on the role of the state in the R.O.C.'s economic development.

The third view of the causative basis of the R.O.C.'s success is in accord with Milton Friedman's thought and is the position taken by Professor Fei when he says that "The economic miracle of the four dragons (including Taiwan) was primarily a story of the success of a competitive market system," and that Chiang Ching-kuo's emphasis, first as Premier and later as President, on price stability was "far more important" than the Ten Major Construction Projects and other state efforts to build up the infrastructure. (Unless otherwise noted, all quotations are from Professor Fei's paper.)

Yet there is also a fourth, more eclectic, perspective on modern economic growth in not only Taiwan but also the rest of the world. If I am correct, this is the view of Professor Ramon H. Myers, and it was a view generally agreed on at the Conference on the Wealth of Nations in the 20th Century, held 7-8 March 1990 at the Hoover Institution, where experts compared notes about economic success or failure in Brazil, Columbia, Egypt, Syria, Ghana, Malawi, North and South Korea, India, Pakistan, and P.R.C., the R.O.C., the U.S.S.R., and, to some extent, Western Europe and the United States. Their consensus, if I am reporting it accurately, was that economic success has stemmed not only from respect for the free marketplace and "conservative" economic policies of the sort Professor Fei recommends but also from some or all of a variety of other factors, such as government efforts to build up the infrastructure and improve human capital, policies slowing population growth, the international context, political stability, situational factors, such as the relatively small size of a society, and culturally inherited patterns.

Thus, it is not clear to me that Taiwan's success can be explained without emphasizing the importance of not only the market system but also a variety of phenomena, such as land reform, state investment in education and in the infrastructure, state efforts—successful indeed—to persuade people to have fewer children (*i-ko hai-tzu pu suan shao, liang-ko hai-tzu ch'ia-ch'ia hao*), the cultural inheritance, and so on. Moreover, Professor Fei himself is somewhat eclectic, since he actually emphasizes not only the efficacy of the market mechanism but also "the superiority" of China's "human resources," due, as he says, to its "cultural heritage."

How effective would the market mechanism have been in Taiwan without this cultural heritage?

Still more, how effective would it have been without continuous intellectual, educational, and political efforts, since the days of Yen Fu, K'ang Yu'wei, Liang Ch'i-ch'ao, and Sun Yat-sen, to *revise* this cultural heritage in the light of the goal of modernization? After all, Chinese culture has been important but so also has been this process of cultural revision. There now tends to be a rough consensus bridging the Taiwan Straits regarding which aspects of the inherited culture are functional, which aspects, dysfunctional, relative to the shared goal of modernization.

Thus on the functional side are the traditional emphasis on family cohesion, frugality and savings, self-reliance, good manners, and other values Professor Fei has astutely noted in some of his writing, such as the idea of being a good loser. Professor Ying-shih Yü and others have also contributed to this list, especially by noting the Confucian emphasis on individual dignity and moral autonomy. On the dysfunctional side—Mainlanders speak of *feng-chien i-tu* (the poisons inherited from the feudal era)—are excessive ceremonial expenses, the desire for too many children, the excessive emphasis on the authority of the old and the male, the tendency of the rich to switch from asceticism to conspicuous consumption, particularism as the failure to care about the larger public or national good, traditional cognitive modes incompatible with modern analytical approaches to the natural and the political worlds, exploitative kinds of bureaucratic and patron-client relations, and so on. Modernization anywhere in China, especially insofar as modernization depends (as Professor Fei emphasizes) on dynamically exploring the "frontiers" of technology and science, could hardly have taken place without efforts to sort out such functional and dysfunctional factors, to agree in identifying them, and then to work at preserving the functional ones, minimizing the dysfunctional.

If, then, we want to evaluate the role of the state in Taiwan with regard to modernization, we need also to ask how this process of cultural revision was carried out. Was it necessary to avoid extreme ideologies either failing to criticize the tradition effectively or iconoclastically throwing out the baby with the bath? Once an effective ideological attitude toward the tradition was formulated, was the state needed to propagate this formulation and effectively to revise the inherited tradition, even if its efforts came under fire as "politicizing and vulgarizing" Confucian values? Because I think the answer to both questions is "yes," I highly value the way that the Sunist state in Taiwan in fact furthered cultural revision and so facilitated economic modernization. Such a governmental role goes far beyond merely minimizing interference with the marketplace. Free of state interference but still mired in traditional attitudes, the market economy in Taiwan would no doubt have stayed under the control of *Ch'a-pu-to hsien-sheng* (Mr. A-little-off-doesn't-matter).

Those of us who were in Taiwan in the 1950s and 1960s still remember him well! Who dealing back then with Mr. A-little-off-doesn't-matter would have been led to admire the ethos of the traditional Chinese market economy? Where then were all those efficient entrepreneurs and magnificent infrastructural facilities inherited from the era of Japanese colonialism? No one then said: "Given the wonders of China's traditional economic culture and the magnificent infrastructure inherited from the Japanese, Taiwan's economy will greatly progress within a few decades!" On the contrary, gloom was in the air, and many wondered whether the economy would survive the end of U.S. economic aid. The economic success that later occurred, in other words, was a surprise.

Professor Fei ascribes this surprise mainly to the government's surprising ability increasingly to stop interfering with the workings of the market, and his point is not easy to refute. Yet even this thesis of his thus identifies two causative factors: market competition and a change in political attitudes and institutions curbing political desires to channel wealth into the hands of the state and its clients. Such a political change cannot be taken for granted. It has not been effected in many developing countries, and in the 1950s, many observers were certain it would not happen in Taiwan.

Thus, even according to Professor Fei's theory, the evolution of the state has been a major aspect of Taiwan's economic modernization, not only the rise of the market. At the same time, however, the state's contribution to economic development seems to have entailed much more than merely withdrawing from the marketplace.

III

Turning from the question of the causative basis of the R.O.C.'s economic success to that of policy recommendations, Professor Fei urges putting primacy on reducing still further any state interference with free competition in the marketplace. He seems to base this recommendation on three reasons. First, as just noted, he holds that since 1945, whatever success the Taiwan economy has enjoyed was primarily due to this element of free competition. As I have tried to argue, however, this theory about the causative basis of Taiwan's economic success is open to question.

Second, Professor Fei believes that as a general principle, if the market system can operate perfectly without government interference, it can provide "solutions to three basic economic issues—production *efficiency*, distributional *justice*, and defense against economic *instability*—that, after all require solution in any viable society."[1] Basic to this thesis is Professor Fei's assumption that given a perfect system of market competition, "a significant portion of the total population can be motivated by an incentive of self-interest to devote their time, energy and talent to creative activities ... that will be socially beneficial in bringing about *progress* in the direction of a new and better world." Thus, pursuing his self-interest, the individual will realize his "inner potential" in a socially constructive way, and society will "constantly renew itself with vitality."

Now, the market is good, but is it that good? Professor Fei's view of it is close to that of thinkers like F. A. Hayek and Robert Nozick, but the thesis that unrestrained market competition results in social justice has been much attacked: "in a world where there is evidence of major and often increasing inequalities between classes, cultures, sexes, and regions, it is hard to see how liberty—liberty to develop one's own tastes, views, talents and ends—could in fact be realized if we do not consider a far broader range of conditions than Hayek's analysis allows."[2]

For instance, since 1985, the free play of the market in Taiwan has so inflated real estate prices that it has become often impossible for the average wage earner to buy a house or condominium. If this situation continues, will the R.O.C. continue being able to boast of "growth with equity"? Could the R.O.C. have made this boast in the first place had not its famous land reform politically redistributed property rights pertaining to farm land, interfering with the free play of supply and demand?

Besides the problem of economic justice, the free play of the market has often had a toxic effect on ecological conditions. Nor should the question of civilizational values be overlooked (jen-wen chu-i). For instance, commercial enterprises often have no respect for the grandeur of nature. Because people will pay to fly low in airplanes over the Grand Canyon, the silent majesty of that spectacle has been destroyed. That is not a minor matter. Professor Fei wants to reduce or eliminate the R.O.C.'s import tax on foreign cars, but will Taipei be helped by more foreign cars creating more traffic jams and air pollution or by a combination of less traffic and more civilized cab drivers?

To be sure, lovers of combustion engines may disagree with my definition of a civilized society. Such disagreement, however, does not invalidate my basic point: Society resolves such disagreements about the nature of civilization and aesthetic needs one way or another, and there is no natural law or other obvious principle of justice demanding that it rely on the profit motive to resolve them.

Again, Professor Fei equates the "vitality" of a society with the constant acquisition of new products, but a society based on such consumerism is not necessarily aesthetically viable or otherwise desirable. Most basically, he views self-interest as necessarily leading to "socially beneficial" activities, but this is a most dubious premise. Would Professor Fei just leave urban development to speculators and real estate developers? Were the U.S. businessmen selling steel to Japan on the eve of Pearl Harbor doing something "socially beneficial"? The U.S. businessmen who export chemicals to Latin America needed to produce cocaine are benefitting themselves, cocaine producers, exporters, and consumers, but does that count as "socially beneficial"? How about the businessmen selling advanced military technology to Libya and Iraq? Does Professor Fei really want to put the world in charge of businessmen free to "compete" with each other in any way they can? Does he really believe such a world accords with the Confucian values he so respects?

I cannot question Professor Fei's economics, but in writing this kind of paper, he has turned from economics to social philosophy, positing that the market, if allowed to work freely, overcomes human frailty. This view clashes with common sense. It reminds one of Hsu Fu-kuan's view that democratic political procedures necessarily lead to political decisions free of subjective, selfish bias.[3] Neither view, I believe, is based on an a posteriori study of how people have historically acted; both are based on an a priori belief that people in the future will be smarter and more moral than they are today if only a certain institutional change can be made. I agree with Professor Chang Hao that such optimism stems from the traditional Chinese lack of a sufficient *yu-an i-shih yü mini-chu ch'uan-t'ung* (awareness of the dark side of life).[4] Thus, I do not think it prudent to base the institutional design of a society on such a utopian faith in the possibility of a public life—whether economic or political—largely free of human frailty. As Robert Bellah and John Dunn have noted, the translation of self-interest into virtue is no simple matter.

Finally, Professor Fei's recommendation that government interference in the marketplace be minimized is based also on his view that Taiwan's experience in 1962-80 has "demonstrated conclusively that 'economics by political demand' is not consistent with the requirement of structural flexibility of a modern technological society." He has in mind especially the "bureaucratic ranking of industries," which was "the foundation of the income transfer strategy through which the income of victimized social groups (the consumers and workers) was transferred routinely to an urban entrepreneurial class that was politically favored and patronized." Thus the P.R.C. leaders, in trying (allegedly) to "carry out a program of total economic reform that rejects the doctrinaire position of the centralism of command of public enterprises . . . have much to learn from the experience of *in Taiwan.*"

Yet it is precisely during this period of "failure" that what Professor Fei and others call an "economic miracle" occurred in Taiwan. In other words, the governmental interference Professor Fei deplores did not prevent the occurrence of this "miracle." After all, the Walter Galenson book with Simon Kuznets' praise for Taiwan's economic development was published in 1979. And Simon Kuznets, as Professor Fei has not tired of reminding us, won a Nobel Prize. I do not see, therefore, how the Taiwan experience in 1962-1980 proves that the kind of governmental intervention which then occurred is a serious impediment to economic growth.

To be sure, Professor Fei could be arguing that had this governmental intervention been eliminated, Taiwan's economic development would have been still more miraculous. Yet being not miraculous enough is hardly the same as "failure."

Moreover, to tell the P.R.C. leaders that they should learn from the "failures" of the R.O.C. is likely to inflate further the already unbearable arrogance and complacency of that incompetent and shameless political gang. I think this kind of inflation is as undesirable as is the kind Professor Fei has warned against. These Communists should instead be told to wake up to the frightening reality of their miserable institutions and to try to copy the design of the Taiwan economy by basically endorsing uncontrolled prices and private property.

After all, they have three options: 1) to fail the way they already have failed for so long; 2) to "fail" the way Taiwan did, thus enormously improving the lot of their people; or 3) to surpass Taiwan's performance. Is the third option practical? Is even the second on the horizon? With all due respect, I must say it is chimerical to suggest that the P.R.C. now aim to surpass the R.O.C.'s economic performance. Can one learn to run before one can walk? Should we urge a beginning student of calligraphy to avoid the "failures" of Yü Yu-jen? Moreover, according to Professor Jan Prybyla, under "the post-Tiananmen leadership, marketization and privatization of the system are clinically dead."[5]

I thus cannot but raise questions about Professor Fei's recommendation that R.O.C. policy in future years just focus on minimizing intervention in the marketplace. Why cannot we distinguish between undesirable intervention—e.g., building up a large state sector, the inflationary policies Professor Fei criticizes—and desirable intervention, such as land reform, investments in infrastructure, investments in human capital, and ecological policies?

IV

It seems to me that, in principle at least, the approach of Dr. Sun Yat-sen was precisely to emphasize both respect for the marketplace and constructive state intervention. If so, then, his views do not seem outdated and are not necessarily refuted by Professor Fei's critique. They are the views that have been central to R.O.C.'s economic policy since 1950 and, as mentioned above, they seem close to that consensus developed at the recent Hoover Institution Conference on "The Wealth of Nations in the 20th Century."

They are also in some harmony with traditional Chinese economic norms. True, Professor Fei has rightly emphasized that traditional Chinese culture in many ways has meshed with the demands of free enterprise. Yet Confucius was not Milton Friedman. No ideal was more basic to Confucian thought than the well-field system (*ching-t'ien*), which precisely combined the idea of private ownership with that of state-imposed parameters limiting private enterprise. I would hope that something like the well-field system can be used in Taipei now to straighten out the inequities of the real estate situation and restore "growth with equity!" The "golden mean" (*chung-yung*) comes to mind. The KMT impulse to intervene in the marketplace no doubt is rightly deplored by Professor Fei as having sometimes gone too far, but is altogether eliminating this impulse the answer? "Not going far enough" is as bad as "going too far," is it not (*kuo-erh pu-chi*)?

Moreover, in weighing Dr. Sun's economic philosophy, I think we have to take into account that it was not a purely differentiated philosophical project, formulating economic principles unconnected to moral-political principles. If a government is to act in an economically efficient way, it must be legitimized and stable, and we cannot say that political stability and moral legitimacy are goals always and necessarily compatible with maximizing economic efficiency. Perhaps they would be if man were the ideally rational animal depicted in so much economic theory as well as modern and traditional Chinese political thought. A more complex, "darker" picture of human motivations is needed, however, when we deal with economic-political realities, and the Sunist philosophy has indeed been sensitive to this point.

Yet Professor Fei's thought does highlight an extremely important aspect of modern Chinese political thought. So far as I can see, not one major modern Chinese ideology has fully legitimized capitalism. Sunism is no exception, even though it accommodates itself to some degree of capitalism. This modern Chinese bias against capitalism, moreover, can be rooted in Confucian thought, as already indicated. After all, despite Mencius's emphasis on the common people's need for *heng-ch'an* (permanent possession of a material basis for living), there was no traditional Chinese philosopher who, like Locke or Rousseau, made protection of private property or the raison d'être of the state. Yet it is clear that private property and capitalism have been of supreme importance in the economic development of Taiwan. Therefore, there indeed is an incongruence between this crucial fact and Sunist philosophy, and Professor Fei's thought can be seen as a legitimate reaction to this incongruence.

Modern China, in other words, has produced thinkers like Professor Fei seeking the formulation of a political philosophy more in accord with valid principles of economics. Moreover, his views certainly coincide with those of many R.O.C. businessmen, who also often deplore governmental interference in their affairs and are critical of Sunism. Thus Professor Fei has addressed a major modern Chinese issue that the liberal and humanistic scholars in Hong Kong, the United States, and Taipei have largely if not entirely failed to deal with. Just because this issue is so important, however, it seems undesirable to move from undue suspicion of capitalism to undue exaltation of it.

Just how Chiang Ching-kuo viewed this issue, however, is still not clear. Professor Fei sees President Chiang's economic thought and policies as part of a process of increasingly understanding the need to minimize state interference with the market, but does this thesis project Professor Fei's vision of the economy into President

Thomas A. Metzger

Chiang's mind? Dearth of information about the latter has forced this panel to focus instead on Professor Fei's highly interesting and significant views.

ENDNOTES

1. See John C. H. Fei, "The Chinese Market System in a Historical Perspective," in *The Second Conference on Modern Chinese Economic History* (3 vols.; Taipei: The Institute of Economics, Academia Sinica, 1989), I:34.

2. See David Held, *Models of Democracy* (Stanford: Stanford University Press, 1987), pp. 253-254.

3. See his *Hsueh-shu yü cheng-chih-chih chien* (Between the Realms of Scholarship and Government; Taipei: T'ai-wan hsueh-sheng shu-chü, 1980), pp. 125-126.

4. See his *Yu-an i-shih yü min-chu ch'uan-t'ung* (Awareness of the Dark Side of Life and the Democratic Tradition) (Taipei: Lien-ching ch'u-pan shih-yeh kung-ssu, 1989).

5. See *The American Asian Review* 8:1 (spring 1990), p. 75.

CHAPTER FIVE

CCK and Society: Institutional Leadership and Social Development on Taiwan

Edwin Winckler

INTRODUCTION

Social development in Taiwan under Chiang Ching-kuo (CCK) is a challenging topic. What is social development? What did CCK have to do with it?

Social development is neither so clearly formulated nor so widely understood as economic or even political development. However, American comparativists are increasingly researching the social bases of political and economic development, the politics of why countries have the social programs they do, and the impact of social policy on social development. Social strength has contributed to Taiwan's postwar political stability and economic growth, and Taiwan has displayed exceptional social stability amid exceptionally rapid social change. Meanwhile Nationalist ideology states high social goals and prescribes state programs for achieving them. However, Nationalist social strategy has been largely indirect, through economic development. This combination deserves more attention.

CCK's role in Nationalist social policy is even more obscure than his role in political or even economic policy. Nationalist ideology prescribed some social goals and strategies, but what the

Nationalists actually did on Taiwan changed much over time. CCK's own role changed too. As policy-implementer, he personally ran some of Taiwan's largest social programs, the Youth Corps and Veterans Services. As policymaker, he displayed a continuing concern for socializing youth and aiding the disadvantaged. As policy-overseer, he allowed gradual formulation of social policies and an increasing priority for them on Taiwan's political agenda. An account of this requires addressing questions of institutional leadership and policy process on postwar Taiwan that also deserve more attention.

Given this definition of the problem, the paper proceeds as follows. The first section extracts a conceptualization of social development on Taiwan from contending western approaches—liberal, radical, and conservative. The second section sketches the political background of social policy on Taiwan—leadership, institutions and instruments. The three sections after that trace the postwar development of three levels of social policy— supranational, national, and subnational. Such comprehensive treatment is necessary to capture the full sweep of Taiwan's postwar social development and the true nature of Nationalist social policy. The conclusion returns briefly to the question of CCK's role.

This paper is a spinoff from a book about Taiwan's postwar development (early = 1945-1960, middle = 1960-1975, late = 1975-1990). Both book and paper are premature because we still lack descriptions of most policy politics on postwar Taiwan. My aim is mainly to identify some processes that deserve further research. The world cannot study "the Taiwan model" until we know realistically what it is and how it occurred.

SOCIAL DEVELOPMENT

Identifying CCK's role in Taiwan's social development requires considering alternative approaches to social development, social policy, and the relation between them.

Social policy means different things to different people, and all of these have played a role in Nationalist policy. Meanings range from very broad and indirect to very narrow and direct, roughly the sequence in which Nationalist social policy itself has developed. The broadest definition, of indirect social policy, is simply the statement of social goals themselves, on the assumption that this is a worthwhile activity in itself and will somehow contribute to the realization of these goals, even in the absence of more concrete measures to realize them. Such exhortation has always been a characteristic of Nationalist social policy, but has gradually decreased relative to other measures. A middle indirect definition is the strategy of pursuing social goals by promoting other kinds of development, usually economic. This was the main Nationalist strategy, a highly successful one, throughout the postwar period. The narrowest definition of indirect social policy is analysis of the social impact of these other programs to maximize their contribution to social welfare. Taiwan's capacity for such analysis, on the part of both state and society, has gradually increased.

The broadest definition of direct social policy is all state policies toward social processes of any kind—immigration and emigration, social and spatial mobility, community and family. Like all countries, Taiwan has had such policies, more conscious and more coordinated than in most. A middle direct definition is social programs for providing social benefits—state rather than market provision of medicare, education, and housing. Relative to comparable countries, the Nationalist state has been conservative about funding such programs, but they have gradually increased, though mostly for state personnel, not mass publics. The narrowest and most direct definition of social policy is "social work" on "social problems"—remedial measures for correcting failures in processes that normally take care of themselves. The Nationalist state has been conservative about funding these too, but due to the success of its indirect strategies, the failures have been relatively few and declining.

Western thought contains three ideological orientations toward these alternatives and how to explain them—liberal, radical, and conservative. All three have "classical" versions analyzing the European transition from agricultural to industrial society, and "revised" versions treating the later maturation and globalization of western capitalism. We briefly review these because each contributes to our analysis, and because each of these too has contributed to Nationalist policy. For each ideology we briefly state how it analyzes social development, what social policies it prescribes, and how it explains what social programs actually occur, noting the relevance of these in Taiwan.

Liberal. The liberal approach is the most widely assumed, by both American and Chinese scholars.

Liberal analyses of development regard the "social" largely as a residue of private behavior left after industrialization transfers major political and economic functions from family to state and firm. Classical liberalism was optimistic that equal participation by rational individuals in free markets would support most individuals and maintain the system. Social policy should just promote education and regulate abuses. Nevertheless, industrialism made it decreasingly feasible for the family to guarantee social security from cradle to grave. By the 20th century, revised liberalism advocated a larger state social role, but still to save capitalism, not to replace it. Less developed countries were likely to repeat the experience of more developed countries—both the necessity and the feasibility of state social programs would increase with the increase in per capita product accompanying industrialization.

Traditional Chinese thought contained few liberal premises, but traditional Chinese society contained many liberal practices. China's late-traditional state could not effectively regulate China's large early-modern markets, leaving guilds and families much de facto liberty. Some modern Chinese intellectuals absorbed some liberal social ideals, such as land reform and mass education, but were unable to implement them much in tumultuous Republican China.

Postwar Western *liberal prescriptions for social policy* still avoid state interference in market processes, intervening mainly to take remedial measures if the market fails. At the supranational level liberalism downplays any relationship of emigrants to their country of origin, favors free flow of persons across international borders, and promotes the melting of differences of ethnic origin. At the national level liberalism leaves demographic, occupational, and spatial outcomes largely to the decisions of individuals; necessary social programs should be implemented through market principles if possible. At the subnational level, liberalism promotes individualism, leaving the organization of community and family to individual practice.

Postwar Nationalist social policy, despite its overall conservatism, does contain some liberal elements. It continued the traditional Chinese freedom of social and spatial mobility. It promoted mass social welfare indirectly, through economic development, which became increasingly marketized.

Liberal explanations of social programs emphasize mass modernization. Democracy allows all social groups to demand state social services, tending to produce roughly the same array of services in all societies. Electoral cycles affect when programs are introduced, and electoral considerations affect how they are funded. Transposed to the global level, the liberal model anticipates that social programs from advanced countries will be diffused to backward countries as they achieve the economic preconditions for implementing them. Indeed, the liberal model promotes such diffusion through international agencies, to improve the prospects for capitalism and democracy.

The overall trajectory of Nationalist social policy broadly conforms to these liberal expectations. Rise in per capita produce was a precondition for expansion of social programs. Democratization was an impetus to their introduction. Nevertheless, the liberal model leaves much unexplained about Taiwan—the continued centrality of the state, why and how it formulated social policies and when and how it implemented them. Moreover, the international diffusion component of the liberal model actually works in reverse, since the growing problems of Western welfare programs made Nationalist policymakers avoid them.

Radical. The radical approach raises many useful questions about Taiwan.

Radical analyses of development use the "social" to expose the relationship between politics and economics. In the 19th century, classical Marxism argued that mass market mechanisms concealed elite political power. In the 20th century social democracy used mass political power to direct market processes to social purposes. What was "social" was the problem of paying the full cost of the labor force throughout its life cycle. Classical Marxism said capitalists paid wages too low to cover all the costs of the "social reproduction" of capitalism, displacing them onto workers. Social democrats transferred these costs to the state, which covered them by taxing citizens in proportion to their incomes, and by pooling risk on insurance principles.

Sun Yat-sen evaluated these radical analyses, rejecting Marxism and favoring social democracy. He considered the Nationalist state responsible for promoting equal ownership of land and capital, and for guaranteeing minimal access to food, clothing, shelter, and transport. If the private market failed, the state should promote cooperatives, or produce and distribute these necessities itself.

Thus the *radical prescriptions for social policy* eventually relevant to postwar Taiwan are those of postwar Western social democracy. At the supranational level this permits some state management of social flows and ethnic relations. At the national level it encourages a shareout of welfare costs between capital, labor, and state. At the subnational level it means extensive programs for maintaining communities, families, and individuals.

Postwar Nationalist social policy largely followed Sun Yat-sen's social democratic ideas. Some worked well, such as land reform and infrastructure construction. Others were less effective, such as rural community development and urban land reform.

As for *radical explanation of social programs,* classical Marxism assumed that capitalists would block them, but social-democratic mass movements obtained them anyway. Consequently a main task for revised Marxism is explaining why. Its answer is that the state does whatever the further development of capitalism requires. Social democracy is really a victory not for workers but for capitalists—a way to have the state subsidize labor and sustain sales. Even apparently progressive social democratic programs such as educational expansion, environmental protection, and urban renewal just reflect the needs of high technology and commercial services. Imperialism is a way of displacing social costs onto other societies (low wages, women workers) and their states (tax holidays, infrastructure provision). For contemporary radical globalism, the relevant unit for explaining national social programs is the capitalist world-system. The social policies of peripheral states will serve the needs of core, not peripheral, societies. Peripheral areas will adopt core social ideals long before they have the material base to implement them, exacerbating tension between state and society.

All this has much application to Taiwan. Collaboration between Western advisers and Nationalist technocrats reversed initial Nationalist antipathy to capitalism. Successive social policies paved the way for successive phases of capitalist development—particularly rural land reform, and the successive expansions of primary, secondary, and tertiary education. Nevertheless, Taiwan's social outcomes are much better than most radical analysis would expect.

Conservative. The conservative approach is most appropriate to Taiwan.

The *conservative analysis of development* considers the "social" a historically specific legacy of institutions and practices that inform and integrate other sectors. Perpetuation of this valuable tradition requires continuous attention from both state and society. Classical Western conservatives, reacting against the industrial and democratic revolutions, defended traditional social elites and promoted traditional mass morality. Among the contributions of local elites was implementation of social policy—private charity to relieve distress, if only to preserve social stability. With modernization, conservative states still encouraged private philanthropy, but assumed some welfare functions, again to avoid social unrest.

Traditional Chinese social policy was predominantly conservative, the state relieving disasters, in collaboration with local elites, to prevent disorder. Modern Nationalist ideology contains many conservative elements, regretting the decline in social cohesion accompanying the transition from agricultural to industrial society. Postwar Nationalist policy has largely counted on society meeting its own social needs.

Conservative prescriptions for social policy believe the state should help society, but are not optimistic that resources will be sufficient, or confident that the state is the best way to distribute them. At the supranational level conservative states retain ties with emigrants, strongly regulate border flows, and discourage entrance of new ethnicities. At the national level, the state should regulate the quantity and quality of population, limit educational opportunities to occupational prospects, and manage the use of national space. At the subnational level, the state promotes forms of community solidarity, family socialization, and individual obligation that support the state. Except for spatial development, Nationalist social policy largely corresponds to this profile.

Conservative explanations of social programs emphasize state role and cultural values. State leaders, acting on their ideologies, initiate social programs, not only in authoritarian, but also in democratic regimes. Among the least developed countries, social programs may serve mainly key state personnel—prewar colonial administrators or postwar national officials. Thereafter state leaders may expand social programs purposefully, as part of state-sponsored development. Or, state bureaus may expand social programs haphazardly, adding incrementally to existing capacities. The particular combination of social programs in each country reflects its sociocultural characteristics, and sociocultural exchanges within subglobal regions like East Asia.

This conservative scenario too largely fits Taiwan. Japan adopted the German conservative-statist-scientific approach, which Chinese carried to the Republican mainland, and the Japanese implemented on prewar Taiwan. Postwar, the Nationalist leadership reaffirmed Sunist social goals and the Nationalist party drafted social programs, without significant popular input. For most of the postwar period, most direct social programs served the state, particularly the military. Another conservative institution, the Chinese family, provided most social services to most Taiwanese. However, the conservative model too requires elaboration. State leaders did not always do what their ideology dictated (economic organization), and sometimes did the opposite (population policy). Some state policies were largely dictated from abroad, as radical globalism emphasizes. The goals and roles of the state itself were eventually themselves transformed, as liberal modernization theory expects.

INSTITUTIONAL LEADERSHIP

Identifying CCK's role in social policy requires knowing the nature of institutional leadership and its relation to social policy on Taiwan.

Leadership as institution. A first relevant meaning of "institutional leadership" is that within the Nationalist state personal leadership was the dominant institution—the system was more Leaderist than Leninist. It combined leaderist precedents from the imperial period with leaderist improvisations and borrowings of the Republican period, with the leaderist legacy of the Japanese governor-general's office, with still further leaderist innovations on postwar Taiwan. The institutionalization of personal leadership was partly through constitutional provisions and ministries, partly through extraconstitutional enactments and agencies, and partly through informal political alliances and personal networks.

Thus it was the Leader's prerogative to pontificate about social ideals. Sun Yat-sen left formal ideological guidance. However, among Sun's three principles, social welfare came after external independence and internal sovereignty, and then consisted mostly of economic development, not social programs. Chiang Kai-shek elaborated Sun's incomplete welfare chapters, and particularly associated himself with expansion of education. However, his budgets too placed external security and national development above social welfare. Chiang Ching-kuo was personally the most populist of the Nationalists' first three leaders, a quality expressed in actions not words, by frequently visiting ordinary people. However, social policy appeared as only one of twelve items in the second set of major projects under CCK's administration, which also were largely devoted to military-industrial construction.

The Leader's supremacy was based on numerous details—ideological, institutional, policy, and personal—that in turn constrained the Leader himself. Among these constraints were principled social commitments. These included ideas such as Sun's "people's livelihood," social policies mandated by the 1946 Nationalist constitution (educational spending), and Chiang Kai-shek's 1954 "supplements" (eugenics, happiness). However, these commitments also included practical requirements such as the Nationalists' political obligation to maintain mainlanders who had fled with them to Taiwan, and their prudential obligation to promote the welfare of Taiwanese as well. Apprenticeship in such constraints qualified CCK to lead the Nationalist state and made him successful at doing so. CCK's problem was to appear as custodian of this intricate legacy while at the same time advancing it. He spoke the required generalities but acted quietly on specifics.

A final aspect of personal leadership worth mentioning is the Leader's personal associates and staff. Chiang Kai-shek's main premier Ch'en Ch'eng was personally associated with land reform, the Nationalists' major early social accomplishment. CCK's choice of premiers expressed and constrained his priorities—developmental technocrat Sun Yun-suan and fiscal conservative Yu Kuo-hua. Evidently there were no "czars" for social policy, or ideologists elaborating Nationalist social theory.

Leadership over institutions. A second meaning of institutional leadership is that the Leader builds institutions and assigns them tasks. As an authoritarian regime, the Nationalist state falls into three sectors—security (external and internal), development (economic and civil affairs), and legitimation (party and parliaments). On the mainland, there was a Ministry of Social Affairs that drafted developmental social goals, but served mostly security functions. On Taiwan, the Nationalist state contains three tiers: extraconstitutional staff agencies helping the Leader manage the state, constitutional line-ministries of the central government, and the largely parallel line-departments of the provincial government. On Taiwan, social administration has remained mostly at the relatively impecunious provincial level, in such departments as Health, Education, and Social Affairs. There has been a central ministry of education, and since 1971 a central agency for health. However, there has been no central ministry for social affairs, which in principle has fallen under the Ministry of Interior, one of the least influential ministries. The main problem with most Nationalist social administration has been low budgetary priority and administrative status, and overstaffing with underqualified and underpaid personnel, who were prevented from accomplishing much by procedures intended more to secure control than to promote efficiency.

Consequently in practice most major social programs were designed by extraconstitutional staff agencies of the central government. In the early period, the joint American-Nationalist Rural Reconstruction Commission (JCRR) supervised most social measures, mostly in public health, because most program funds came from American aid, and because most of the population remained rural. In the middle period the central planning commission (CIED) took social measures in support of urban-industrial development, in particular shifting the focus of educational planning from political indoctrination toward vocational training, to facilitate the transfer of labor from agriculture to industry. By the late period the central planning commission (CEPD) had developed some capacity for socio-spatial planning, trying to equalize access to social services for Taiwan's increasingly metropolitanized population. Another extraconstitutional agency, the Research and Evaluation Committee, also claimed some role in social policy.

CCK began his own career on Taiwan in internal security (from 1949), then expanded into external security (from 1957), later into economic affairs (from 1969), and finally to everything else (during the 1970s). The security aspects of Nationalist social policy probably were always subject to his inspection, at first through informal authorization from his father, later formally through the National Security Bureau and Political Warfare Department. However, he probably did not have much opportunity to review the economic-developmental and party-political aspects of mass social programs until 1969, when he became vice premier of the government and effectively assistant party leader.

Leadership through institutions. Also characteristic of an authoritarian regime, the Nationalist state included mass organizations for control of society—occupational associations, youth corps, women's organizations and so on. Such control is an authoritarian regime's most basic direct social policy, and these mass organizations are its principal channels for implementing it. Such organizations also constitute important power bases within authoritarian states, providing staging areas within which power contenders can cultivate their own policies and personnel. Such auxiliary organizations were long one of CCK's main responsibilities, an important stepping-stone to power and his most direct experience of social administration. CCK headed the Youth Corps, to provide young people with ideological indoctrination, vocational training, and leisure opportunities. A key source of CCK's political aides, the Youth Corps pioneered the "service attitude" toward public administration that they later extended to other institutions on CCK's behalf, itself a significant form of social policy. CCK also headed RETSER, to provide economic employment and social services to demobilized servicemen. It too was a source of technocrats and patronage for CCK.

The Nationalists also fielded some mass social programs, whose policy instruments evolved over time with the increase of resources and change in target groups. In the early period, when the society was still rural, and the state felt it had virtually no money to spend, the Nationalists relied mostly on a "normative" approach. They reaffirmed the goals of the earlier New Life Movement on the mainland—using proper material environment to reinforce proper spiritual attitudes. However, they did not really do much to implement them, except for the JCRR's public health measures and pilot community projects. In the middle period, when the government had a little money to spend, direct mass social policy became mixed normative and remunerative. Community development—mobilizing the population for minor community improvements—became the main instrumentality of direct Nationalist social policy. However, as actually implemented, community development became largely a way of distributing minor public works contracts to favored rural political clients, with little impact on either material or spiritual welfare. In the late period, the government had more money to spend and better social planning, but remained cautious about the effectiveness and expense of mass social programs. It limited itself to a "remedial" approach in which the government did really begin to assist the very small portion of the population whose basic needs were not met by market and networks.

A third institutional channel for delivering social policy to society has been the use of major organizations with general functions, like the party and police, for social purposes. By the later postwar period, at the lower administrative levels, they made a significant contribution. At its mass level the Nationalist party, particularly after 1969, performed many welfare functions, expediting the solution of local social problems brought to its attention, and identifying new ones. These constituency services had electoral motives, but they served society nonetheless. The police too adopted an increasingly sophisticated role in society, as much forceful social workers treating modernization disorders as centurions repressing social disorder. Police academies remain an important source for social administrators.

CCK'S ROLE

We now briefly survey three levels of Nationalist social policy—supranational, national, and subnational—identifying programs in which CCK was involved.

Supranational. Externally derived Nationalist social policy includes three domains—relations with Chinese communities outside Taiwan, current flows of persons across international borders and, on Taiwan, relations between persons of different external origin. Among these, CCK's contribution to ethnic relations on Taiwan is most conspicuous.

Chinese communities outside Taiwan include the Chinese on the mainland, mainland emigrants around the world, and recent emigrants from Taiwan to North America. Social relations with Chinese on the mainland has been, of course, a difficult issue for Nationalist policy, which long forbade social intercourse between Taiwan and the Chinese mainland. In the early period, CCK was quite involved in mainland operations, particularly psychological warfare broadcasts, which he continued to modernize in the middle period. (Later one of his sons ran the relevant broadcasting organization.) It was during CCK's administration that the Nationalists' policy of "no contact" was strained by a few Nationalist veterans on the mainland whom the PRC allowed to apply for admission to Taiwan, and from the many aging mainlander veterans on Taiwan who wished to revisit their native places before they died. Placing good security above bad publicity, CCK long stood by "no entrance." However, at the end, he declared family visits a humanitarian issue, unleashing a tide of visits to the PRC by both mainlanders and Taiwanese.

CCK had no conspicuous involvement with Chinese in Southeast Asia, which had declined in importance by the time he became vice-premier. Nevertheless, his administrations continued a modest commitment—retaining Overseas Chinese National Legislators, modernizing relevant publications, and building a college for Overseas Chinese students on Taiwan. In contrast, relations with Chinese in North America became more important. Aside from their increasing numbers, these populations had links back to Taiwan politics and forward to American politics that required watching. One can only assume that CCK supervised such surveillance. This need not mean that he authorized some of the unfortunate incidents that occurred during his administration, such as the murder in San Francisco of his biographer, or the death on Taiwan of a visiting professor.

The second domain of external social policy concerns current flows of persons across international borders—for defense, diplomacy, business, employment, tourism, or study. Restrictive Nationalist policy toward outgoing Chinese was set in the early postwar period. As usual, the Nationalist bottom line was security—keeping young men at home long enough to perform their military service, then allowing some to go abroad to avoid their becoming malcontents. Economic reasons for restrictiveness included conserving foreign exchange and discouraging brain drain. CCK's administrations retained most of these policies, though with increasing prosperity, they did gradually lift restrictions on foreign travel. Taiwan's switch from internally to externally oriented economic development around 1960 required relaxing restrictions on foreigners, which the security sector opposed. Presumably CCK played a role, representing the views of the security sector to policymakers and vice versa. However, exactly what his role was remains only a tantalizing question.

The third domain of "external" society policy, ethnicity, includes relations between Taiwanese and mainlanders and Han treatment of aborigines. The most salient ethnic distinction on

Taiwan is of course that between Taiwanese and mainlanders, the latter themselves of diverse origins, dialect and status. The main cleavage is political-economic—elite mainlanders have greater access to state power than elite Taiwanese, and mass mainlanders are more dependent on the state for employment and benefits than mass Taiwanese, who have their families to take care of them. CCK did more than any other person to bridge this gap. At the elite level, he personally promoted "Taiwanization" of state institutions at all levels. At the mass level, he personally visited ordinary Taiwanese in all walks of life and all parts of the island, to show his affection and concern. Near the end of his career he summoned Taiwan's regional elites and announced that, having spent nearly 40 years on Taiwan, he considered himself Taiwanese. CCK did not publicly indicate special interest in aborigines. However, he did personally supervise early road construction across aborigine areas, and during his administration the provincial Department of Social Affairs commissioned a major study of possible social programs for aborigines.

National. National social policy includes three domains—demographic, stratificational, and spatial.

Demographic policy includes public health, population, and medicare, which came on the policy agenda in the early, middle, and late periods, respectively. Consequently the main involvement of CCK's administrations was with medicare. During his administrations, public health addressed certain infections peculiar to Taiwan (hepatitis B), but began shifting its attention to occupational and environmental health. Population policy, originally pro-natalist (to produce soldiers for defense), then long anti-natalist (to limit the pressure of population on development), at the end of the postwar period suddenly again became pro-natalist (so there would be enough working people to support retired people). In medicare, because of rising income and aging population, during the late period of CCK's administrations the government began expanding medical coverage. Revenues and personnel became sufficient to begin "cloning" elite public medical facilities into an island-wide network. Medical insurance (mostly for state personnel, but also for some workers), became one of the main components of rising central government social expenditures.

Stratification policy involves class, occupation, and education. CCK's main impact on class was to reinforce the dominance of political over economic or cultural stratification. CCK's own view of the relationship between government and people combined traditional paternalism with modern populism. Privately he dissociated himself from business elites and publicly he associated himself with working masses. His suspicion of private business tycoons may have impeded their penetration of state policy making but could not, in the end, prevent it.

As regards occupational structure, Nationalist policy facilitated Taiwan's gradual transition from labor-intensive to skill-intensive industries, both favorable to employment and income distribution. If CCK had a distinctive role, it was association in the middle period with the main counterpoint to this dominant trend—tentative promotion of capital-intensive heavy industry, which produced mixed results. In the later period, CCK acceded to a shift away from uncompetitive, polluting heavy industry toward energy-efficient hi-tech industry.

Education is one of a state's largest and most direct impacts on national social structure. For political stability and economic efficiency, Nationalist policy long restricted the amount of upper-middle and higher education, to keep educational attainment congruent with occupational structure. By the late postwar period development had created both the demand and the resources for more tertiary education, which CCK's administrations began cautiously to expand. They also attempted minor reforms in Taiwan's fair but rigid college entrance examinations.

Spatial policy includes regional planning, urban planning, and housing construction. At the regional level, when CCK began participating in economic planning around 1969, he associated himself with efforts to improve regional balance by accelerating the development of central and eastern harbors. However, he evidently postponed plans to facilitate the decentralization of the Taipei and Kaohsiung metropolitan regions through government construction of new satellite towns. Evidently he also endorsed rather nominal and general land-use planning for the island as a whole, rather than detailed regulation of the rapid growth within metropolitan regions.

At the urban level, the main problems have been underregulation of private development and underprovision of public infrastructure. The water and electrical supplies are good; zoning and density controls are haphazard; traffic order and congestion are terrible; most human sewage remains untreated; and industrial pollutants accumulate. Some of this results from government policy, mediated by CCK's choice of economic lieutenants. Neither productionist Sun Yun-suan nor financialist Yu Kuo-hua favored large expenditures on social amenities. A particularly fateful choice was the decision at midpoint to develop a private auto industry (to upgrade the troop-transport, machine-tool, and export-earning capabilities of Taiwan's military-industrial complex) instead of public mass transit. The Nationalists have left housing largely to private saving and private construction, which worked remarkably well. It was only after CCK's demise that housing costs in big cities became a political issue.

Subnational. Subnational social policy includes communities, families, and individuals.

As regards communities, as noted above, in the middle period, the Nationalists made community development their main direct rural social program. However, implementation was unsatisfactory. Later CCK endorsed trying again with better design and more resources. Despite his populism, CCK avoided public association with traditional community religious rituals. Instead, CCK's later administration constructed county-level centers for modern cultural activities.

The Chinese family performs three crucial functions for the Nationalist state—socializing youth, employing adults, and sustaining elderly. However, for most of the postwar period, the Nationalists took the family largely for granted. Only in the later postwar period did they begin considering a family policy to encourage the family to continue performing these vital functions. While associating himself with traditional family virtues, evidently CCK did not consider them alone sufficient—he promoted the Youth Corps to give young people additional guidance.

As for individual behavior, the main concern of Nationalist social policy is to prevent what it regards as social deviance, to preserve public safety and social morality. The social problems that have concerned Nationalist, like Western, social planners are violence, gambling, and sex. (Drinking, smoking, and watching television, discouraged by some Western states, on Taiwan are served by government monopolies.) Despite some reports of accommodation with organized crime, Nationalist authorities conducted periodic sweeps against it, presumably under CCK's direction. For youth, unconventional behavior includes adolescent antics and juvenile delinquency. Formerly restricted on Taiwan to such manifestations as long hair and social dancing, during the late period it escalated to include motorcycle racing and even unconventional sexuality. For adults, late period allegations of deviance focused on syndicated gambling and commercialized sex. Some of these indulgences, such as youth motorcycle racing and adult chain lotteries, caught policymakers' attention. Like other conservative Nationalist elders, CCK deplored them, with little effect.

CONCLUSION

Further assessment of CCK's role in Nationalist social policy would require fieldwork specifically on that role, which I have not undertaken systematically. All this paper has done is to identify some of the intersections between his career and relevant social processes. Most direct Nationalist social programs fall in the later postwar period under his administration, first as Premier, then as President. Much of the explanation for this timing is developmental, contingent on rising government revenues. Given CCK's reticence, even interviewing might not reveal his instructions. The most one can say at this distance is that it seems unlikely, if he had opposed such policies, that his administration would have adopted them. Moreover, he helped unleash the political democratization that made such policies inevitable, and identified himself with humanist and populist values that would support them.

This leads to a final reflection on the relation between institutional leadership and social policy. Critical Western perspectives, and many Taiwan critics, justifiably highlight the gap between Nationalist ideological pretensions and their actual social programs, a gap that closed only gradually across the postwar period. However, traditional Chinese administrative theory, and some modern organization theory as well, argue that exemplifying values is a major function of leadership, with an efficacy of its own. In any case, realizing ideals takes time, and in retrospect the postwar period appears brief. Aristotle distinguished between malign and benign states, those that act in the interests of the rulers versus those that act in the interests of the ruled. On postwar Taiwan the interests of both were served, not something that one can take for granted. CCK helped shift the balance from rulers toward ruled, with effects that will persist long into the post-postwar period.

NOTES

SOCIAL DEVELOPMENT

The best introduction to Third World social policy is Hardiman and Midgley 1982. On **comparativists' explanations of social policy**, a superb introduction is Skocpol and Amenta 1986. On contending approaches to Taiwan's development in general, see Winckler and Greenhalgh eds. 1988.

For overviews of **social development in Taiwan**, see Institute of Economics 1976, Ahern and Gates eds. 1981, Chu ed. 1981, Chiu and Chang eds. 1986, China Forum ed. 1986, NTU-LAW 1986 (National Taiwan University, College of Law), Yang and Chiu eds. 1987, and NTU-SOC 1987 (National Taiwan University, Department of Sociology). For a PRC summary see Lin 1988.

For introductions to **social policy on Taiwan**, see Yang and Yeh eds. 1979, DOI 1981 (provincial Department of Information), Ling 1983, Yang and Yeh eds. 1984, KMT 1984, and DOI 1985. For measurements of social inputs and outcomes, see Kao ed. 1985 and DOSA 1988 (provincial Department of Social Affairs). For general evaluations of Nationalist social policy see Peng 1984 and the multiple annual volumes of social assessment by leading intellectuals published in the mid-1980s by several Taiwan publishers. On public perceptions of social well-being see Yang and Chiu eds. 1987:61-158. For preliminary comparison of Taiwan's social policies with those of other countries, see Wang and others 1982 and Liu 1982.

Liberal. Among major liberal analyses of social policy were Wilensky 1975 and Jackman 1975.

Radical. Major radical analyses of social policy include Miliband 1969, Poulantzas 1973, O'Connor 1973, Gough 1979, and Offe 1984.

Conservative. The major recent work is that of Skocpol and associates—see Weir ed. 1988.

INSTITUTIONAL LEADERSHIP

Leaderism as an institution. For comparative institutional analysis see Perlmutter 1981. On Sunist ideology see Gregor and others 1981.

Leadership over institutions. For the institutional structure of the Nationalist state on Taiwan, see Winckler 1984 and Winckler in Feldman ed. 1988. On JCRR see Yager 1988, on CIECD/CEPD see Winckler 1974. For CCK's career see Liu 1984, Liu 1985, Li 1987, and Winckler in Winckler and Greenhalgh eds. 1988 (elite power struggles). I have taken the memorial volumes issued in 1988 by his funeral committee as the definitive official public representation of his career.

Leadership through institutions. On mass organizations in authoritarian regimes, see again Perlmutter 1981. Overviews of Nationalist social policy area cited above under SOCIAL DEVELOPMENT.

CCK'S ROLE

Supranational social policy. For the concept of supranational society, and the diffusion of social policies within it, see Meyer and Hannan eds. 1979.

Diaspora. For comparative framework see Sheffer ed. 1986. On Nationalist policy toward Overseas Chinese see OCAC 1981, 1983 (Overseas Chinese Affairs Commission).

Flows. For comparative framework see McNeill and Adams eds. 1978 and Alonso ed. 1987.

Ethnicity. For a general introduction see Tsai in Yang and Chiu eds. For **aborigine** history see Shepherd 1981; on social policy toward aborigines see Li in Yang and Yeh eds. 1984. On

Taiwanese-mainlander relations see Gates in Ahern and Gates eds. 1981, Institute of Ethnology, 1989, and the current work of Marshall Johnson.

National social policy. On interplay of the demographic, social, and spatial transitions see Oshima 1987.

Demographic transition. On **public health,** for early measures see the chapter in Yager 1988. For subsequent developments see MOH, Health statistics, periodic (Ministry of Health; has interpretive introduction). On environmental health, Huang in Yang and Yeh eds. 1984 and Hsiao ed. 1989; on consumer health Hsiao in Yang and Yeh eds. 1984. For **population,** on Japanese period see Barclay 1954, on Nationalist intervention see Freedman and Takeshita 1969. For subsequent developments see periodic updates by Freedman and associates in the Population Council journal *Studies in Family Planning* and Freedman, 1986. On **medicare** see Chang and Li, in DOI 1981, KMT 1984:209-250, DOI 1985:17-44, and Pierson et al. eds. 1982.

Social transition. On **stratification** see Gates in Ahern and Gates eds. 1981, Chiu and Chang eds. 1986:299-378 and Sheu in NTU-SOC 1987 (National Taiwan University, Department of Sociology). On **occupational** change and labor relations see Yu in DOI 1981, Chang, and Lin, in Yang and Yeh eds. 1984, KMT 1984:67-108. DOI 1985:263-280 and DOSA 1988:216-319; on manpower planning, vocational training, and employment guidance, see Yu in DOI 1981, KMT 1985:263-280, and CEPD 1981; on labor Chang in Yang and Yeh eds. 1984, Zeigler 1988 and DOSA:274-285; on working-class life see Gates 1987. On **education** see Yang in Yang and Yeh eds. 1984; Chiu, and Chan and Chan, in NTU-SOC 1987; and MOE Educational statistics, annual (Ministry of Education). On the indoctrinational effects of Nationalist education see Wilson 1970 and 1974, and Meyers 1988 and 1988.

Spatial transition: On postwar **regional**-urban development see Speare and others 1988; on Nationalist regional policy see Winckler 1974. The main regional and policy studies on Taiwan are those of

CEPD-UDD (Urban Development Division of the central planning agency), directly by Ts'ai Hsiun-hsiung, particularly his studies of "living circles" for delivering social services. For more on **urban** policy see Tang and Lin in DOI 1981, Ch'en in Yang and Yeh eds. 1984, DOI 1985:239-262, and Taiwan 1988. On **housing** see Wu in DOI 1981.

Subnational social policy. For overviews see Yang and Yeh eds. 1984 and DOSA 1988.

Community. On early community **development** see Yager 1988. For a critical evaluation of middle period Nationalist community development programs see Apthorpe 1972. For later retrospectives see Hsiao in DOI 1981, KMT 1984:47-66. DOI 1985:331-340, Liao in Yang and Yeh eds. 1984, and DOSA 1988:28-61. On **religion** as a policy problem see Fan in GIO 1981, Li in Yang and Yeh eds. 1984 (who says it is not that much of a problem) and Chiu and Yao in Chiu and Chang eds. 1986 (where it is grouped with crime!). On rural community **leadership** see Stavis 1974 and Jacobs 1980. On cooperatives see DOI 1985:191-210 and DOSA 1988:182-215, on associations DOI 1985:281-288.

Family. On **welfare** support in general see DOI 1985 45-82 and 172-190. On the family as a policy issue see Lin in Yang and Yeh eds. 1984. On children and **youth** see Huang in DOI 1981, KMT 1984 (141-178 and DOSA 1988:62-131; on socialization Bond ed. 1986. On the **elderly** (including veterans homes and social support in general) see Lin DOI 1981, KMT 1984:109-140 and 179-208, Chang in Yang and Yeh eds. 1984, and DOSA 1988:132-176.

Individual. In general, see the section on individuals in Yang and Yeh eds. 1984 and in Yang and Chiu eds. 1987:159-298. On the general problem of **leisure** Wen in Yang and Yeh eds. 1984 and Wen in Yang and Chiu eds. 1987. On **juvenile delinquency** see Ma in Yang and Yeh eds. 1984. On **adult crime** see Huang, and Chiu, in Yang and Yeh eds. 1984.

REFERENCES

Ahern, Emily and Hill Gates eds. 1981. *The Anthropology of Taiwanese Society*. Stanford: Stanford University Press.

Alonso, William ed. 1987. *Population in an Interacting World*. Cambridge: Harvard University Press.

Apthorpe, Raymond 1972. *Social Development Planning Studies*. Taipei: U.N. Mission to the ROC for Community Development.

Barclay, George W. 1954. *Colonial* Development and Population in Taiwan. Princeton: Princeton University Press.

Bond, Michael Harris ed. 1966. *The Psychology of the Chinese People*. Hong Kong: Oxford University Press.

CEPD 1981. *Studies in Manpower Planning*. Taipei: Committee for Economic Planning and Development. In Chinese.

Chang, Kwang-chih et al. eds. 1989. *Anthropological Studies of the Taiwan Area: Accomplishments and Prospects*. Taipei: Department of Anthropology, National Taiwan University.

Chiang Kai-shek 1954. Two supplementary chapters. In *The Three Principles of the People*. Taipei: China Publishing.

China Forum ed. 1986. *Taiwan Area Social Change and Cultural Development*. Taipei: China Forum. In Chinese.

Chiu, Hai-yuan and Ing-hua Chang eds. 1986. *Social and Cultural Change in Taiwan*. Nankang: Institute of Ethnography, Academica Sinica, 2 vols. In Chinese.

Chu, Ling-lou ed. 1981. *Our Country's Social Development*. Taipei: Tung-ta.

DOI 1981. *Social Development.* Taichung: Department of Information, Taiwan Provincial Government. In Chinese.

DOI 1985. *Social Stability and Social Welfare.* Taichung: Department of Information, Taiwan Provincial Government. In Chinese.

DOSA annual. *Social Statistics of Taiwan Province.* Taichung: Department of Social Affairs, Taiwan Provincial Government.

DOSA 1988. *Social Statistics of Taiwan Province for Forty Years.* Taichung: Department of Social Affairs, Taiwan Provincial Government.

Feldman, Harvey ed. 1988. *Taiwan in a Time of Transition.* New York: Paragon.

Freedman, Ronald 1986. "Policy Options After the Demographic Transition: The Case of Taiwan." *Population and Development Review* 12, 1 (March).

Freedman, Ronald and John Takeshita 1969. *Family Planning in Taiwan.* Princeton: Princeton University Press.

Gates, Hill 1987. *Chinese Work-class Lives: Getting By in Taiwan.* Ithaca: Cornell.

Gold, Thomas 1986. *State and Society in the Taiwan Miracle.* Armonk: Sharpe.

Gough, I. 1979. *The Political Economy of the Welfare State.* London: Macmillan.

Gregor, A. James et al. 1981. *Ideology and Development: Sun Yat-sen and the Economic History of Taiwan.* Berkeley: Center for Chinese Studies.

Hardiman, Margaret and James Midgley 1982. *The Social Dimension of Development.* New York: Wiley.

Hsiao, Michael Hsin-huang ed. 1989. *Taiwan 2000: Balancing Economic Growth and Environmental Protection.* Taipei: Institute of Ethnology, Academica Sinica, 1989.

Institute of Economics 1976. *Conference on Population and Economic Development in Taiwan.* Taipei: IOE, Academica Sinica.

Institute of Ethnology 1989. Conference on ethnicity on Taiwan.

Jackman, Robert 1975. *Politics and Social Equality: A Comparative Analysis.* New York, Wiley.

Jacobs, Bruce 1980. *Local Politics in a Rural Chinese Cultural Setting.* Canberra: Contemporary China Centre, Research School of Pacific Studies, Australian National University.

Kao, Hsi-chun ed. 1985. *First Social Report on the Republic of China.* Taipei: Ming Der Foundation. In Chinese.

KMT 1984. *Social Development.* Taipei: Culture Commission, Nationalist Party. In Chinese.

Li Yuan-pien 1987. *Chiang Ching-kuo and Taiwan.* Hong Kong: Wide Angle Press.

Lin Yau-ch'in 1988. *Taiwan Society.* Xiamen: Lujiang Press.

Ling, Shih-lin 1983. *Social Policy and Social Legislation.* Taipei: Yung-ta.

Liu, Chi-chu 1982. *Comparative Research on Chinese and Foreign Social Policy.* Taipei: Central Cultural Service.

Liu, Sheng-tun ed. 1984. *Sunist Social Development.* Taipei: Chung-cheng.

Liu, Henry 1984. *Biography of Chiang Ching-kuo.* Los Angeles: American Tribune. In Chinese.

Liu, Yung-hsi 1985. *Thirty Years of Chiang Ching-kuo on Taiwan.* Hong Kong: Ta-lien.

McNeil, William and Ruth Adams eds. 1978. *Human Migration: Patterns and Policies.* Bloomington: Indiana University Press.

Meyer, John and Patrick Hannan eds. 1979. *National Development and the World System.* Chicago: University of Chicago Press.

Meyers, Jeffrey 1988. "Moral Education in Taiwan." *Comparative Education Review* 32, 1 20-38.

Meyers, Jeffrey 1988. "Teaching Morality in Taiwan Schools: The Message of the Textbooks. *The Chinese Quarterly* 114 (June) 267-284.

Miliband, Ralph 1969. *The State in Capitalist Society.* New York: Basic Books.

MOE annual. *Educational Statistics of the Republic of China.* Taipei: Ministry of Education.

MOH annual. *Health Statistics of the Republic of China.* Taipei: Ministry of Health.

NTU-LAW 1986. *Symposium on Social Change In Taiwan.* Taipei: School of Law, National Taiwan University.

NTU-SOC 1987. International conference on Taiwan as a newly industrialized society. Taipei: Department of sociology, National Taiwan University.

OCAC 1983. *Ten Years of Overseas Chinese Work.* Taipei: Overseas Chinese Affairs Commission. In Chinese.

O'Connor, James 1973. *The Fiscal Crisis of the State.* New York: St. Martin's Press.

Offe, Claus 1984. *Contradictions of the Welfare State.* Cambridge: MIT.

Oshima, Harry 1987. *Economic Development in Monsoon Asia.* Tokyo: University of Tokyo Press.

Peng, Huai-chen 1977. *Problems of the Taiwan Experience.* Taipei: Tung-ch'a.

Perlmutter, Amos 1981. *Authoritarianism: A Comparative Institutional Analysis.* New Haven: Yale University Press.

Pierson, Richard et al. eds. 1982. *The Future of Health Services in Taiwan, ROC.* New York: American Bureau for Medical Advancement in China.

Poulantzas, Nicos 1973. *Classes in Contemporary Capitalism.* London: Verso.

Sheffer, Gabriel ed. 1986. *Modern Diasporas in International Politics.* London: Croon Helm.

Shepherd, John 1981. *Plains Aborigines and Chinese Settlers on the Taiwan Frontier in the Seventeenth and Eighteenth Centuries.* Ph.D. dissertation, Anthropology, Stanford.

Skocpol, Theda and Edwin Amenta 1986. "States and Social Policies." In *Annual Review of Sociology* 12, 1331-157.

Speare, Alden et al. 1988. *Urbanization and Development: The Rural-Urban Transition in Taiwan.* Boulder: Westview, 1988.

Stavis, Benedict 1974. *Rural Local Governance and Agricultural Development in Taiwan.* Ithaca: Rural Development Committee, Cornell University.

Taiwan 1988. Special issue on urban development. *Taiwan: A Radical Quarterly* (Summer-Autumn). In Chinese.

Wang, Wei-lin et al. 1982. *Comparative Research on Chinese and Foreign Social Problems*. Taipei: Central cultural services. In Chinese.

Weir, Margaret et al. eds. 1988. *The Politics of Social Policy in the United States*.

Wilensky, Harold 1975. *The Welfare State and Equality*. Berkeley: University of California Press.

Wilson, Richard 1970. *Learning to be Chinese: The Political Socialization of Children in Taiwan*. Cambridge: MIT.

Wilson, Richard 1974. *The Moral State*. New York: Free Press.

Winckler, Edwin 1974. *Regional Development on Taiwan: Case Studies and Organizational Analysis*. Ph.D., Government, Harvard.

Winckler, Edwin 1984. "Institutionalization and Participation on Taiwan: From Hard to Soft Authoritarianism?" *The China Quarterly* 99 (September), 481-499.

Winckler, Edwin and Susan Greenhalgh eds. 1988. *Contending Approaches to the Political Economy of Taiwan*. Armonk: Sharpe.

Yager, Joseph 1988. *Transforming Agriculture in Taiwan: The Experience of the JCRR*. Ithaca: Cornell.

Yang, Kuo-chu and Chiu Hai-yuan eds. 1987. *Taiwanese Society in Transition*. Nankang: Institute of Ethnology, 1987. In Chinese.

Yang, Kuo-chu and Ch'i-cheng Yeh eds. 1979 and 1984. *Taiwan Social Problems*. Taipei: Chiu-liu. In Chinese.

Zeigler, Harmon 1988. *Pluralism, Corporation and Confucianism.* Philadelphia: Temple University Press, 1988.

CHAPTER SIX

Chiang Ching-Kuo's Policies Toward Mainland China and the Outside World

RALPH N. CLOUGH

The period during which Chiang Ching-kuo was the paramount leader in Taiwan was a time of severe stress for the Republic of China (ROC). The United States, which had been Taiwan's protector against the military threat from the People's Republic of China (PRC) and the primary supporter of the ROC's international position, radically changed its posture toward the PRC from hostility to friendliness. Many other countries followed the U.S. example. The PRC made a succession of conciliatory overtures toward the authorities and people of Taiwan, while continuing to assert its determination to resort to force if necessary to bring about the reunification of Taiwan with the mainland.

Thus, in terms of external relations, Chiang Ching-kuo had to respond to three principal challenges: (1) to retain as strong a relationship as possible with the United States, despite the U.S. determination to establish formal diplomatic relations with the PRC; (2) to respond firmly to the PRC's combination of threats, conciliatory gestures, and demands for negotiations; and (3) to find ways to counter the PRC's efforts to isolate the ROC in the international community. In many respects, the relationship with the United States was the key to the ROC's ability to stand firm against PRC pressures. Consequently, the period of Chiang Ching-kuo's rule can conveniently be treated as consisting of two phases, 1972-78, before the United States formally recognized the PRC and 1979-88, after the United States had severed diplomatic relations with the ROC and ended the mutual security treaty.

PHASE 1: 1972-78

Chiang Ching-kuo became premier in May 1972, the culmination of a long period of grooming for that high position. He was particularly well qualified in terms of his experience in carrying out policies toward the China mainland. During the 1950s and early 1960s, under his father's overall direction, he had supervised all intelligence and paramilitary activities against the mainland. In 1964 he became vice minister of defense and was promoted to minister the following year. In 1969 he became vice premier, thus, for the first time, undertaking supervisory responsibilities extending beyond defense and intelligence matters to include the gamut of domestic and foreign policy.

Chiang Ching-kuo placed a high value on the Confucian virtue of loyalty to his father. He customarily sought his guidance on all important issues. But in July 1972 Chiang Kai-shek fell ill with pneumonia and never thereafter fully recovered his health. During the months that he spent in the Veterans Hospital, Chiang Ching-kuo visited him at least twice a day to brief him and get his instructions. By the time that the father died, in 1975, Chiang Ching-kuo had fully established his position as the next paramount leader, even though Vice President Yen Chia-kan, the constitutional successor, became president. Chiang Ching-kuo was elected chairman of the Kuomintang (KMT) and in 1978, when Yen's term expired, he was elected president of the ROC. He carried on his father's tradition of "strongman government," retaining in his own hands the principal personnel appointments and the final decision on major policy issues.

Chiang Ching-kuo's principal adviser on foreign relations was Shen Chang-huan. Shen, who had an M.A. from the University of Michigan, had been Chiang Kai-shek's personal secretary from 1945 to 1948 and government spokesman from 1950 to 1953. He then entered upon a lengthy career in foreign affairs, as vice minister of foreign affairs (1953-59), ambassador to Spain (1959-60), minister of foreign affairs (1960-66), ambassador to the Holy See (1966-69), and ambassador to Thailand (1969-72). Thus, when he served as Chiang Ching-kuo's foreign minister from 1972 to 1978, he had already had long and varied experience in the field. His strong anticommunist convictions, his determination not to deviate from the one-China position in the ROC's diplomatic relations, and the high value he placed on maintaining as close relations as possible with the United States coincided closely with the views of his leader.

ROC Relations with the United States

When Chiang Ching-kuo became premier in 1972, the ROC had already lost its seat in the United Nations. Support among the members for continuing to exclude the PRC had been on the decline for years. With President Nixon's announcement in July 1971 that he would visit the PRC and the abandonment of U.S. opposition to PRC seating in the United Nations, remaining support for the ROC crumbled. The General Assembly voted to admit the PRC in place of the ROC.

President Nixon's visit to the PRC in February 1972 was another blow to ROC confidence in its U.S. connection. In April 1970, when Chiang Ching-kuo had visited the United States in his capacity as vice premier, he had been told by Nixon: "I can assure you that the United States will always honor its treaty obligations and, to use a colloquial expression, I will never sell you down the river."[1]

Then came the Shanghai Communiqué, in which the United States agreed with the PRC to facilitate trade, contacts, and exchanges with that country. More ominously, from the ROC's viewpoint, the United States agreed to send a senior U.S. representative to Peking from time to time "to further the normalization of relations between the two countries." Moreover, the United States declared that it would progressively reduce its forces and military installations in Taiwan as the tension in the area diminished, with their total withdrawal as the ultimate U.S. objective.[2]

The ROC foreign ministry denounced the agreement between the United States and the PRC as null and void and reiterated the dedication of the ROC to overthrowing the "brutal rule" of the Chinese Communist regime. The foreign ministry's statement declared that far from leading to a relaxation of tension in the Asian-Pacific region, as President Nixon hoped, his visit would have the diametrically opposite effect.[3]

In Washington, Ambassador James Shen sought assurances from President Nixon, National Security Adviser Henry Kissinger, and Secretary of State William Rogers that Nixon's visit to the PRC did not portend a change in U.S. relations with the ROC. Shen received assurances from Nixon himself that the United States was determined to abide by its commitments to the ROC, including the mutual defense treaty, but ROC officials remained uneasy concerning the trend in U.S.-PRC relations.[4]

In early March 1972, reacting to the U.S. rapprochement with the PRC, Foreign Minister Chow Shu-kai resorted to a classic move in alliance diplomacy, threatening to open relations with the principal enemy of its ally. He told American correspondents that the ROC was prepared to explore the possibility of establishing friendlier relations with the Soviet Union. Chow said he envisioned secret talks between Taipei and Moscow on the pattern of the Warsaw talks between Washington and Beijing.

Ambassador Shen, who met with Chiang Kai-shek immediately after the Chow interview and discussed it with him, expressed his conviction afterward that Chow's diplomatic maneuver had not been approved by Chiang. Soon thereafter Chow Shu-kai lost his position as foreign minister.[5] If Chow's ploy did not have Chiang Kai-shek's approval, Chiang Ching-kuo could hardly have known and approved of it. In March 1972 Chiang Kai-shek was still very much in charge and Chiang Ching-kuo was only deputy premier. (He became premier in May 1972.) In his public statements Chiang Ching-kuo consistently declared that the ROC would hold firmly to its anticommunist pattern and remain in the democratic camp. Even during the period of deep disappointment and resentment toward the United States just after Washington established diplomatic relations with the PRC, Chiang Ching-kuo explicitly rejected the idea of seeking military or economic aid or any other relationship with the Soviet Union.[6]

In 1973 another move by the United States justified the uneasiness felt by ROC officials. Washington and Beijing agreed to the establishment of liaison offices in each other's capitals, headed by senior diplomats. Although the liaison offices and their officers were not listed in the official diplomatic lists maintained by the United States and the PRC, they served for most purposes as surrogate embassies. The presence in Washington of PRC diplomats attracted much public and press attention. Before long the PRC liaison office overshadowed the ROC embassy. The head of the liaison office, Huang Zhen, had easier access to the President and the secretary of state than did the ambassador from Taipei.

In 1974 ROC officials were encouraged by the appointment of a senior career diplomat, Leonard Unger, as ambassador to Taipei and by Washington's concurrence in the opening of three new ROC consulates in the United States. A congressional resolution in 1975 sponsored by Representative Dawson Mathis and supported by 218 members of the House of Representatives called on the U.S. government, "while engaged in the lessening of tension with the People's Republic of China, to do nothing to compromise the freedom of our friend and ally, the Republic of China and its people."[7] In a Gallup poll in April 1977, 62 percent of the respondents considered the establishment of diplomatic relations with the PRC as very or fairly important, but only 28 percent favored doing so at the cost of ending diplomatic and defense relations with the ROC. Forty-seven percent were very or fairly strongly opposed to paying that price.[8]

Countering such favorable developments were increasing signs that the United States was moving toward normalization of relations with the PRC, particularly after President Jimmy Carter took office in January 1977. Secretary of State Cyrus Vance visited Beijing in August 1977, followed by National Security Adviser Zbigniew Brzezinski in May 1978. Meanwhile, the higher level official visitors from Washington to Taipei were assistant secretaries of state for East Asian and Pacific affairs, and even these visits were infrequent. The end of the Vietnam War eliminated the need for Taiwan as a support base for operations there, and by 1977 U.S. military personnel stationed in Taiwan had dropped from a high of 10,000 to 1,100. Ambassador Unger warned ROC officials that they should be prepared for the normalization of diplomatic relations between Washington and Beijing.

Chiang Ching-kuo and his senior officials worked tirelessly to convince Americans of the disastrous effects on Taiwan and on East Asia generally that would result from U.S. acceptance of the PRC's three conditions for normalization: ending diplomatic relations and the security treaty with the ROC and withdrawing all U.S. military personnel. ROC officials invited many members of Congress, congressional staffers, and scholars to visit Taiwan, particularly seeking out those who had recently visited the PRC, in order to draw their attention to the higher living standard and greater freedom of the people on Taiwan. But the attraction of mainland China for the people of the United States remained strong, and the Carter administration, like its two predecessors, placed a high value on working out the normalization of Washington-Beijing relations, in order to strengthen the U.S. position relative to the U.S.S.R.

Apprehensive that the United States might yield to Beijing's demand to end the U.S.-ROC security treaty, Chiang Ching-kuo took steps to strengthen the ROC's defense capability. Taiwan's arsenals increased their production of small arms, artillery, artillery shells, and rocket launchers. The co-production on the island of Bell helicopters and F5E fighters began, at first largely from imported components, but gradually increasing the locally manufactured content. In 1976 the ROC bought from the Hughes Aircraft Corporation a sophisticated new radar air defense system to coordinate the command and control of both interceptor aircraft and surface-to-air missiles. The ROC required little assistance from the United States in maintaining and overhauling military aircraft, tanks, and naval vessels. It would be dependent on the United States, however, for many years to come for parts for its relatively sophisticated military equipment and for advanced weapons.

The ROC was now able to buy military equipment from the United States, either through the U.S. government's Foreign Military Sales program or directly from commercial manufacturers; it was no longer dependent on U.S. military aid. Consequently, the

ROC expanded its procurement office in the United States and gave much attention to the cultivation of a network of useful contacts in the U.S. government and the Congress, and among arms manufacturers. If the security treaty ended, it would be more essential than ever to keep the pipeline of needed military equipment flowing.

Economic ties between Taiwan and the United States grew rapidly during the 1970s. Between 1971 and 1978 two-way trade increased from $1.3 billion to $7.4 billion.[9] In 1973 the United States established a trade center in Taipei and in 1975 businessmen in the United States and Taiwan set up the U.S.-ROC Economic Council, which met each year, alternately in the two countries, to promote trade and investment. U.S. Export-Import Bank loans reached $1.2 billion in 1975, with an additional $700 million in guarantees, the bank's largest exposure in any country except Brazil. By 1976, 200 American companies belonged to the American Chamber of Commerce in Taipei, as compared to only 60 in 1972.[10] Thus, as Chiang Ching-kuo became increasingly concerned about the state of political relations between the United States and the ROC, he could view with satisfaction the growth of economic relations, which would provide a solid foundation for a continuing substantive relationship between the two countries even though diplomatic relations were severed.

ROC Relations with Mainland China

The breakthrough in U.S.-PRC relations in 1972 shocked the government and people of Taiwan and encouraged the PRC to redouble its efforts to induce the Taiwan authorities to negotiate. PRC propaganda warned the people of Taiwan that the United States could not be relied on and sought to convince them that the "liberation" of Taiwan was inevitable. The PRC stepped up the number of broadcasts from former KMT officials addressed to their ex-colleagues who had fled to Taiwan, seeking to persuade them that they would be well treated if they contributed to the historic reunification of Taiwan with the mainland.

In February 1973 the PRC held a meeting in Beijing commemorating the 1947 uprising of Taiwanese against the KMT authorities. Liao Cheng-zhi, a member of the Chinese Communist party's Central Committee, called on the civilian and military officials of the "Chiang Kai-shek clique" to work for the reunification of the motherland. He pledged that if they did so, the PRC would treat them "with due respect and forgive them for their past wrongdoings—however serious those were." A former Nationalist general, Fu Tso-yi, who had surrendered Beijing to Chinese Communist forces and in return had been made a cabinet minister in the new government, appealed to his former associates now in Taiwan, warning them that they could not rely on the United States much longer. He said:

> We are all Chinese . . . why couldn't we talk for the sake of the sacred cause of unifying the motherland? . . . Let us come together and talk, the sooner the better. If you are not prepared to enter into formal talks right away, then send some people to the mainland, openly or secretly, to have a look and visit relatives and friends. You can rest assured that the government will keep the matter secret, keep its word and guarantee your safety and freedom to come and go.[11]

During the 1970s, the PRC began to pay greater attention to the Taiwanese, probably recognizing that their political influence was on the rise, particularly after Chiang Ching-kuo became premier. As early as August 1972, Zhou Enlai discussed Taiwan with a group of overseas Chinese from North America. Zhou stressed the great importance of the role of Taiwanese in the peaceful liberation of Taiwan. He even expressed understanding of the sympathy among overseas Chinese for the Taiwan independence movement, attributing this mistaken attitude to KMT propaganda and the long separation of Taiwan from the mainland. He urged Taiwanese to visit the mainland in order to see with their own eyes the true nature of the popular revolution there. Calling attention to the complexity of the liberation of Taiwan, Zhou emphasized the need for patience and the avoidance of a military solution. He said that the transfer of private enterprise in Taiwan to government ownership would be gradual and would not lower the standard of living on the island. He added that the PRC could negotiate with the existing government for the liberation of Taiwan, but that the regime would have to be removed so that the people of Taiwan could manage their own affairs.[12]

In October 1974 Deng Xiaoping outlined for a group of overseas Chinese and Taiwanese current PRC policy toward the liberation of Taiwan:

> What method should be adopted for the liberation of Taiwan? In general, it is hoped that this can be resolved through peaceful negotiations. However, there is a problem: At present, with Chiang Kai-shek and his son in power, can peaceful negotiations be carried out? Can the negotiations be successful? There are basically no negotiation at present. What should be done if peace is impossible? What other methods could be taken if the peaceful method cannot be carried out? We should not exclude this method! . . . At this state prior consideration is given to the peaceful method. . . . the result at the beginning is not always very great, but the work accumulated little by little will produce an effect.[13]

In 1975 Beijing made a gesture toward Taiwan by releasing over 500 Nationalist prisoners. Nearly 300 of these were senior officials who had been jailed for 25 years or longer. They included government, KMT, and security services officials, as well as military officers with the rank of lieutenant general or major general. The other released personnel were midlevel Nationalist officials or special agents and crew members of ROC ships who were captured between 1962 and 1965 after infiltrating PRC territory. Minister of Public Security Hua Guofeng declared that the release of these "war criminals" would promote "the patriotic struggle of the people of Taiwan against the Chiang Kai-shek clique."[14] The ROC refused to admit any of the senior officials who had spent 25 years in PRC prisons, but did accept back the group of special agents captured in the 1960s. More than half of the latter were Taiwanese, who had belonged to intelligence agencies under Chiang Ching-kuo's direction.

In its efforts to influence Taiwanese, the PRC invited to the mainland many individuals of Taiwan origin living in Japan, the United States, and other parts of the world. Some overseas Taiwanese were invited to take part in sports events, including one group that was designated the "Taiwan delegation" to take part in the Third National Games in September 1975. In Beijing's propaganda during the 1970s, appeals to the Taiwanese and to former Nationalist officials to visit the mainland and work for unification alternated with harsh attacks on the regimes headed by Chiang Kai-shek and Chiang Ching-kuo and depictions of daily life in Taiwan as filled with misery for the masses.

Responsible PRC officials kept alive the threat that military force might be used against Taiwan. In his work report to the National People's Congress in February 1978, Premier Hua Guofeng called on the People's Liberation Army (PLA) to make full preparations for liberating Taiwan.[15] In April 1978 the vice chief of the general staff, Wu Xiuquan, told Japanese visitors that without the use of armed force the liberation of Taiwan would be impossible. He said that the PLA was pushing preparations especially for securing command of the air and sea and in training troops for landing operations.[16]

The ROC's reaction to PRC pressures and inducements during the 1970s was to stand firm, strengthen Taiwan's economy and defenses, and reject negotiations. President Chiang Kai-shek set the tone in his "directive" to the Fourth Plenary Session of the 10th Central Committee of the KMT in November 1973:

> At a time when the people of the world have momentarily lost their way and the moral courage of the anticommunist camp is an at ebb . . . History will record that in this dark age it was the Kuomintang of China which never submitted to the pressure of force nor yielded to temptation, but continued to brave bitter suffering and uphold its principles. . . . It is the clear and firm policy of our party never to "negotiate" with the Chinese Communists and never to "compromise" with them.[17]

In his own "administrative report" to the same meeting, Premier Chiang Ching-kuo echoed his father's sentiments:

> At this moment when people of the world stand at the crossroads, bewildered and without being able to tell right from wrong or to distinguish friends from foes, we shall adhere firmly to our anticommunist position. We shall never deal with the devil. . . . The struggle against communism and for national recovery is our basic national policy and will never be changed under any circumstances. We shall never compromise with the enemy and never negotiate peace with him.[18]

During the 1970s, Chiang Ching-kuo and other ROC officials repeated this basic position again and again. The government relaxed somewhat its ban on imports from the China mainland, permitting a gradual increase in the importation of Chinese medicines and other specialty Chinese products. But the prohibition on travel to and from the China mainland remained in effect. Government spokesmen vehemently denied rumors of secret negotiations between Taipei and Beijing that occasionally circulated in Japan or Hong Kong.

Fighting International Isolation

The ROC's loss of the Security Council and General Assembly seats in the United Nations was a severe blow, because it opened the way for the PRC to force the ROC to withdraw from the seats in other U.N. organizations that it had occupied as the recognized government of China. The ROC soon lost its seat in the Economic and Social Council, UNESCO, WHO, the FAO, and other U.N.-affiliated intergovernmental organizations. Pressing its advantage, the PRC in 1974 prevailed upon the general conference of UNESCO to pass a resolution urging international nongovernmental organizations affiliated with UNESCO to exclude immediately and break all relations with "bodies or elements linked with Chiang Kai-shek." Not all such nongovernmental organizations complied with this resolution, but many did. The ROC managed to hold on to its seats in the World Bank, the International Monetary Fund, and the Asian Development Bank through 1978, as the PRC was not yet prepared to undertake the obligations required of members of these organizations and the members were unwilling to expel the ROC unless the PRC were to become a member.

Many countries followed the example of the U.N. in breaking relations with the ROC and establishing relations with the PRC. One of the first and most important countries to take this step was Japan, which broke relations with Taipei and set up a diplomatic mission in Beijing in 1972. In 1971 the number of countries maintaining relations with Beijing had been about equal to the number that had relations with Taipei, but by February 1973 those recognizing Beijing had already jumped to 85, while those recognizing Taipei had dropped to 39.

Although the ROC lost much ground during the 1970s in its diplomatic relations with foreign countries, its substantive relations with most of these countries expanded decisively. Foreign trade increased from $2.9 billion in 1971 to $23.7 billion in 1978.[19] The economy, stimulated by the rapid rise in exports, continued its strong growth, and there was no slackening in the influx of foreign investment. Foreign banks found Taiwan an attractive place to open branches. Taiwan's larger firms had little difficulty in obtaining foreign currency loans, and some of them began to invest abroad: in the United States, Singapore, Hong Kong, Australia, and Saudi Arabia. Taiwan construction companies signed sizeable contracts for work in the Middle East. Visitors to Taiwan more than doubled from 1971 to 1978.[20]

The ROC succeeded in intensifying its substantive relations with foreign countries, despite its loss of diplomatic relations with most of them, by devising ingenious substitutes for diplomatic relations. The most elaborate arrangement was with Japan, Taiwan's second most important trading partner. The Japanese set up an unofficial organization called the Interchange Association, based in Tokyo, with offices in Taipei and Kaohsiung. ROC authorities established the East Asia Relations Association, based in Taipei, with offices in Tokyo, Osaka, and Fukuoka. The two associations signed an agreement specifying their functions, which included most of the activities normally carried on by diplomatic missions. The associations' offices were staffed mainly by retired diplomats or by other government officials, temporarily released from their official positions. Each government extended to the officials of the association from the other country the rights and privileges essential to the performance of their functions. Other countries established offices in Taipei for the purposes of furthering their national interest and the interests of their citizens. Although none was as elaborate as the Japanese agency, they served the purposes of promoting trade, facilitating travel, and conducting cultural exchanges.

Because foreign trade was Taiwan's life blood, the authorities established in 1970 a private trade promotion organization, the China External Trade Development Council, supported by compulsory donations from exporters. Its offices abroad took the place of official trade missions or commercial attaches in diplomatic missions. By 1978 the Council had a staff of 236 in Taipei and 33 offices overseas.

Thus, the PRC's efforts to isolate the ROC in the international arena failed, except in the narrow sense of formal diplomatic relationships. The ROC, adjusting its international relationships to the peculiar requirements of its unique situation and to the needs and desires of its trading partners, not only survived, but prospered.

Imminent Loss of Diplomatic Relations with the United States

In a speech to the Asia Society in June 1977, Secretary of State Cyrus Vance, shortly before a visit to the PRC, the first by a senior official of the Carter administration, declared that the United States considered friendly relations with the PRC to be a central part of its foreign policy. He said that "policy toward China will continue to be guided by the principles of the Shanghai Communiqué, and on that basis we shall seek to move toward full normalization of relations." Vance made no mention of the ROC in his speech.

ROC Foreign Minister Shen Chang-huan promptly responded in alarm that it was "extremely dangerous for the United States to consider friendly relations with the Chinese Communists to be a central part of its foreign policy." He went on to stress the aggressive designs of the Chinese Communists and warned: "Should the United States choose to recognize the Chinese Communists by abandoning the long-standing friendly relations with the Republic of China, it would not only seriously damage the rights and interests of the Republic of China and jeopardize the security of the 16 million Chinese on Taiwan, but would also violate the lofty ideals upon which the American nation was built and the moral principles emphasized by the Carter administration and thus erode the credibility of the United States among the free peoples the world over."[21]

Chiang Ching-kuo's inaugural address after his election as president in May 1978 reflected the concern felt in Taiwan at the determination of the Carter administration to normalize relations with Beijing. "We are now facing a crucial test of a new era in a new situation," Chiang said. "The fierce conflict confronting us will decide our fate: glory or humiliation, freedom or slavery. So we look toward the struggle with strengthened determination and ever greater certainty of our success."

Chiang viewed the situation in the stark terms of an irreconcilable conflict between "total right" as represented by the ROC and anti-Communist Chinese on the mainland and "total wrong" represented by the Chinese Communist regime. He called for sacrifice to further strengthen Taiwan as the "bastion of national recovery."

Chiang gave international relations only a minor place in his address, urging strengthened relations with free nations, particularly the United States, and warning the United States that pursuing a balance of power strategy against the Soviet Union by building bridges to the Chinese Communists would only result in "letting a wolf in through the back door" while "battling a tiger at the front door."[22]

PHASE 2: 1979-88

As president, Chiang Ching-kuo soon had to make fundamental decisions as to how to react to the U.S. decision to normalize relations with Beijing and how to deal with the proposals for contacts and negotiations made by the Chinese Communists from their strengthened international position. Chu Fu-sung, an experienced diplomat who had served as vice minister of foreign affairs when Shen Chang-huan was minister in the early 1960s, became foreign minister in 1979. Shen Chang-huan, however, continued to be Chiang Ching-kuo's most influential adviser on foreign policy issues from his new position as secretary-general of the National Security Council.

Relations with the United States

Chiang Ching-kuo was roused from bed on 16 December 1978 in order to receive at his residence at 2:30 a.m. U.S. Ambassador Leonard Unger, who informed him that in seven hours President Carter would announce the establishment of diplomatic relations with the PRC and the severance of relations and the ending of the mutual security treaty with the ROC. Chiang hurriedly called an early morning meeting of the standing committee of the KMT's central committee and then issued the strongest condemnation of the United States that the ROC had ever made.

Chiang said that the U.S. decision had "not only seriously damaged the rights and interests of the government and people of the Republic of China, but also had a tremendous adverse impact upon the entire free world." Chiang pointed out that the United States had repeatedly reaffirmed its assurances that it would maintain diplomatic relations with the ROC and honor its treaty commitments. "Now that it has broken the assurance and abrogated the treaty," Chiang declared, "the United States government cannot be expected to have the confidence of any free nation in the future." He referred to the U.S. action as "a great setback to human freedom and democratic institutions" that would be condemned by all freedom-loving and peace-loving people throughout the world.

Chiang urged the people of Taiwan to stand firmly with the government and face adversity with dignity. He pledged again that the ROC would not negotiate with the Chinese Communist regime, would never compromise with communism, nor give up its sacred tasks of recovering the mainland and delivering the compatriots there.[23]

In two days of negotiations in late December 1978 with a delegation headed by Deputy Secretary of State Warren Christopher concerning the relationship between Taiwan and the United States after the termination of formal diplomatic relations, ROC negotiators were unable to win U.S. agreement to government-to-government relations between the two countries. Christopher insisted that representatives must be unofficial, in accordance with the pledge made by President Carter to the PRC. In an interview with the *New York Times* on 30 December, Chiang Ching-kuo continued to insist on governmental relations, but in a full-page advertisement in the *Washington Post* the day before, he had anticipated the need for greater emphasis than in the past on people-to-people relations. His "Message to the American People," accompanied by his photograph, extended Christmas and New Year's greetings and declared that "the change in relations between our governments will make no difference in the friendship of our two peoples. In our hearts we still have confidence in Americans."[24]

After prolonged negotiations in Washington, Vice Foreign Minister H. K. Yang reluctantly agreed to the establishment of the American Institute in Taiwan to represent the United States and the Coordination Council for North American Affairs to represent Taiwan in the conduct of affairs between the two countries. ROC diplomats lobbied vigorously with members of Congress during the drafting of legislation on future relations between the United States and Taiwan. The Taiwan Relations Act (TRA), as signed into law by President Carter in April 1979, was much more favorable to Taiwan than the administration's original draft, although it maintained the principle that relations would be conducted through unofficial means.

Despite the shock and sense of betrayal that caused anti-American demonstrations in the streets of Taipei immediately after Carter's announcement, Chiang Ching-kuo never lost sight of the reality that the future of Taiwan continued to depend heavily on a close association with the United States. He canceled elections scheduled for the week after the U.S. announcement in order to prevent a divisive campaign debate at a moment when order and unity were essential to coping with the crisis. He then sought, through negotiations and lobbying, to minimize the damage to Taiwan from the changed relationship. By May 1979, after the adoption of the TRA, Chiang Ching-kuo felt that the crisis had been surmounted. In an interview with a *Time* magazine correspondent, Chiang said that the situation had improved greatly since January. He stressed the need for access to weapons from the United States and expressed pleasure that the TRA showed continued U.S. concern for Taiwan's stability and security. He said that the ROC and the United States shared many common interests and that he was confident that close people-to-people relations would never be terminated.[25]

Shifting from official to unofficial relations was not easy. Criticism and suspicion of the Carter administration was prevalent in Taiwan. Many thought U.S. representatives too scrupulous in avoiding any appearance of officiality in their dealings with the ROC and too sensitive to criticism from Beijing. In Washington, representatives from Taiwan were suspected of deliberately seeking to display an increasing degree of officiality in their contacts, in order to create friction between Washington and Beijing.

The PRC's proposals in 1979 for trade, travel, and negotiations with Taiwan, and Ye Jianying's 9-point elaboration in 1981, offering a substantial degree of autonomy to Taiwan, created a public relations problem for the ROC in the United States. To many Americans, Beijing's proposals for negotiations seemed reasonable, while the ROC's policy of "no contact, no negotiations, no compromise" seemed unduly rigid. A statement by Premier Y. S. Sun to a group of American scholars in June 1982 somewhat softened the ROC's image of rigidity. Sun envisaged a continued narrowing of the political, economic, social, and cultural gap between the China mainland and Taiwan that would brighten prospects for negotiating a peaceful reunification of Taiwan with China.[26]

Ronald Reagan's election as president in 1980 brought a surge of hope to Taiwan. Reagan had a reputation as a "friend of the ROC," and his campaign speeches had called for the restoration of official relations between Washington and Taipei. ROC officials stepped up the campaign already underway in the last year of the Carter administration for the sale of Taiwan of an advanced fighter aircraft. Beijing reacted strongly to the threatened upgrading of Washington/Taipei relations and the proposed sale of high-performance fighters. The Reagan administration was soon embroiled in a lengthy and difficult negotiation on the issue of arms sales to Taiwan, an issue which had been left unresolved in the agreement on normalization of relations.

In order to prevent the deterioration of relations with the PRC, the U.S. government not only dropped the idea of supplying Taiwan with an advanced fighter, but issued a joint communiqué with the PRC in August 1982 in which it pledged to limit the quality and gradually reduce the quantity of weapons sold to Taiwan. U.S. officials stressed to the Congress that the limitation on weapon sales to Taiwan was predicated on the PRC's declaration in the joint communiqué that its fundamental policy was to strive for a peaceful solution to the Taiwan question and that any change in this peaceful policy on the part of the PRC would cause the United States to reexamine its arms sales position.

The United States also assured the Taiwan authorities that it had not agreed to a date for ending arms sales, had not agreed to prior consultation with the PRC on arms sales, had not agreed to revise the TRA, had not altered its position on sovereignty over Taiwan, would not mediate between Taipei and Beijing, and would not press Taipei to negotiate with Beijing.

Despite these "six assurances," the agreement by the U.S. government with the PRC to limitations on arms sales had a damaging impact on U.S.-Taiwan relations. The ROC government charged that the U.S. government had been tricked by the Chinese Communists into signing an agreement that violated the letter and spirit of the TRA and was aimed at paving the way for a military invasion of Taiwan.[27] Chiang Ching-kuo appealed to his people, in the face of adversity, to strengthen themselves for the trials ahead.[28] Washington-Taipei relations sagged, as commentators in Taiwan gloomily predicted that renewed Chinese Communist pressures in the future would wring out further U.S. concessions.

Chiang Ching-kuo's efforts to maintain close relations with the United States were affected, not only by PRC pressures on the United States, but also by developments in Taiwan's domestic politics. Rising demand by Taiwan's political opposition in the late

1970s for a more democratic political system drew increasing attention among Americans to the KMT's monopoly of power in Taiwan and the repression of dissidents under a martial law regime that had existed since 1949. Many Americans criticized the sentencing to long prison terms of opposition leaders involved in an anti-KMT demonstration in Kaohsiung in 1979. The death in Taiwan under mysterious circumstances of a Taiwanese professor at Carnegie-Mellon University after long interrogation by security officials on his connections with the Taiwan independence movement was the subject of a hearing by the House Foreign Affairs Committee. The hearing produced details of extensive surveillance of Chinese in the United States by KMT agents and caused the committee to warn the Taiwan authorities that intimidation in the United States of persons from Taiwan by such agents could result in restriction on arms sales to Taiwan.[29]

Even more damaging to Taiwan's reputation in the United States was the murder in California in October 1984 of Henry Liu, author of an unflattering biography of Chiang Ching-kuo, by agents of the Intelligence Bureau of the Ministry of National Defense. The ROC sought to contain the damage by sentencing to life imprisonment two members of the Bamboo Gang who had been involved in the murder, and giving life imprisonment also to Wang Hsi-ling, director of the Intelligence Bureau, and shorter terms to two of his associates. Chiang Ching-kuo did not permit his past close association with the Intelligence Bureau to deter him from acting decisively to punish a high official caught in an act that threatened serious damage to U.S.-Taiwan relations.

In late 1986 Chiang made two decisions that would transform Taiwan's domestic politics. He announced that martial law would be lifted and the ban on new political parties ended. While he took these steps primarily in response to domestic political pressures, they were welcomed by Americans and greatly improved Taiwan's image in the United States. Another momentous decision made in late 1987, to allow residents of Taiwan to visit their relatives on the mainland, also had a beneficial effect on U.S.-Taiwan relations.

The principal problems in U.S.-Taiwan relations toward the end of Chiang Ching-kuo's rule were in the trade field. Taiwan was running a large trade surplus with the United States, second only to

Japan's. U.S. pressure on Taiwan to remove barriers to U.S. imports caused resentment in Taiwan, but the government made a series of concessions that met most U.S. demands.

By the time that Chiang died in January 1988, U.S.-Taiwan relations had improved considerably over the low point of the early 1980s. Taiwan's diplomats had learned the advantage of maintaining a low profile. They became skilled at carrying out essential business in Washington in their unofficial capacity. They cultivated a wide range of Americans, not limiting themselves to "friends of the ROC" as in the past. Members of Congress and congressional staff visited Taiwan, along with a stream of state and municipal officials. The Taiwan authorities had come to value the TRA as affording protection and giving Taiwan a unique legal status, which it did not have in other countries where it lacked diplomatic relations.

Keeping relations low key and out of the limelight facilitated the acquisition of needed weapons and parts. The United States interpreted the 1982 communiqué as permitting a very slow decline in the quantity of weapons supplied in terms of real prices, thus not affected by inflation. The United States also permitted the purchase of technology to be used for the production of high-performance fighters and other advanced weapons in Taiwan.

Growing Interchange Between Taiwan and Mainland

The U.S. decision to end the security treaty with Taiwan and break diplomatic relations encouraged the leaders in Beijing to press for negotiations on the unification of Taiwan with the PRC. On 1 January 1979 the Standing Committee of the National Peoples' Congress (NPC) announced a halt in the shelling of the offshore islands and called for talks between the government of the PRC and the Taiwan authorities. The announcement also proposed the opening of trade, transportation, and postal services, and academic, cultural, sports, and technological interchange. In October 1981 Ye Jianying, the chairman of the PRC's Standing Committee, elaborated on the foregoing proposals, offering Taiwan a high degree of autonomy as a special administrative region of the PRC. Taiwan's socioeconomic system, its way of life, and its economic and cultural relations with foreign countries would remain unchanged. Taiwan would retain its armed forces, the central government would not interfere in local affairs, and there would be no encroachment on private property or foreign investment. Ye proposed that representatives of the Chinese Communist party and the KMT meet to discuss these arrangements.

In September 1982 Deng Xiaoping proposed a "one country, two systems" concept as a framework for incorporating Hong Kong, Macao, and Taiwan into the PRC. The constitution adopted in December 1982 contained a provision for the creation of "special administrative regions" with political and economic systems different from those of the rest of the PRC. In September 1984 the PRC reached agreement with the British government on the treatment of Hong Kong as a "special administrative region" after it came under PRC sovereignty in 1987. The PRC appealed again to the Taiwan authorities for negotiations, assuring them that as a "special administrative region" Taiwan would have greater autonomy than Hong Kong.

ROC authorities rejected all proposals for negotiations, holding firmly to their long-established policy of "no contacts, no negotiations, no compromise." In remarks to a national development seminar in 1982 Chiang Ching-kuo spelled out the official rationale for rejecting negotiations:

> We must always remember that while talk may be a rational way to solve problems in the free world, to the Communists it is another form of war.... We have had the bitterest of experiences in this connection. Although there were many causes for this fall of the Chinese mainland, one of the main reasons was the mission of a few politicians and Communist fellow travellers that went to Peking to talk peace with the Communists. To begin with, these "peace talks" brought about internal dissension, blurred our demarcation from the enemy and deprived the nation of its central objective. In other words, we lost our resolve and strength. Now the Chinese Communists are again clamoring for "peace talks".... In fact, they have never changed their aim of

seizing Taiwan and subjugating its people under Communist rule. We therefore refuse to talk with them or enter into any contacts, thereby foiling their plot . . . Our exposure of their conspiracy is not a negative step but a positive and powerful counterblow against their united front tactics.[30]

Although the ROC clung firmly to the "three no's" policy and rejected PRC proposals for direct trade and direct communication and transportation links, indirect unofficial interaction between people on the two sides of the Strait developed rapidly during the 1980s. Scholars from both places met and conversed at international conferences in third countries. Students from Taiwan and the mainland studied side by side at foreign universities. Both governments encouraged such personal contacts, hoping to gain advantage in the rivalry for political influence.

Residents of Taiwan and their relatives on the mainland exchanged letters via Hong Kong, Japan, or the United States. Substantial trade developed, mainly through Hong Kong. Surreptitious visits to mainland relatives occurred with increasing frequency. Fishermen carried on a profitable small-scale barter trade at sea in the Strait.

In May 1986 a China Airlines pilot landed his plane in Guangzhou to defect to the PRC. The ROC wanted to recover the plane and crew, but could not negotiate officially with the PRC without breaching the "three no's" policy. Eventually, negotiation were conducted between China Airlines and the PRC airline, the Civil Aviation Administration of China, thus permitting the ROC to claim that the negotiations had been private, not official.

Chiang Ching-kuo's rejection of official negotiations with the PRC had wide support in Taiwan. Those who had fled to Taiwan from the mainland in 1949 recalled the Chinese Communist slogan: "fight, fight, talk, talk" and generally agreed with Chiang's characterization of Beijing's appeal for negotiations as a united front tactic designed to split and weaken the opposition. Many Taiwanese harbored a suspicion that the mainlander leaders in the KMT might one day strike a deal with Beijing and sell them out. Any softening of Chiang's rigid rejection of negotiations would have fed their suspicion and undermined his support among the Taiwanese.

The reaction among the people of Taiwan to the PRC's proposals for mail exchange, trade, and travel was quite different from their negative reaction to proposals for negotiation on reunification. Many individuals had personal reasons for desiring contact with people on the mainland. They wanted to correspond with their relatives or to visit them. Businessmen wanted to take advantage of profitable opportunities to trade. As indicated above, surreptitious travel and indirect trade increased during the 1980s. The numbers engaged in such technically illegal acts became so large that prosecution of all the violators was impracticable. Selective enforcement of the law by sending to jail a few businessmen or visitors to the mainland was widely seen as unfair discrimination.

Chiang Ching-kuo found himself in a difficult position. His long experience as the supervisor of the ROC's security apparatus, responsible for preventing Chinese Communist infiltration and subversion, conditioned him to be highly resistant to proposals to ease restrictions on travel and trade or to end martial law. His more liberal advisers, such as Y. S. Sun, Y. S. Tsiang, and Ma Chi-chuang, initially were unable to prevail over more conservative officials such as Wang Sheng or Shen Chang-huan.[31] Chiang, who was not consulted in advance concerning Sun's statement to American scholars in June 1982 on the prospects for eventual negotiation with Beijing, firmly reiterated the "three no's" policy at the National Development Seminar in July 1982. But by 1986 pressures were growing both at home and abroad, for liberalizing domestic politics and easing restrictions on travel to and trade with mainland China. Consequently, in October 1986 Chiang announced that martial law and the ban on new political parties would be lifted.

Criticism of the government's rigid ban on contact with the mainland grew louder in 1987. Several KMT legislators pointed out that the exchange of mail and visits to relatives were an open secret. They acknowledged that the government had legitimate security concerns, but argued that the authorities should have more confidence in the people's ability to resist Chinese Communist blandishments. They urged the government as a humanitarian measure to bring regulations in line with reality. Articles by scholars took a similar line. The ban on private contacts could not be enforced and violations promoted disrespect for the law, they wrote. Moreover, the government's proclaimed goal of unifying China under the San Min Chu Yi required contacts so that the people on the mainland could learn about Taiwan's experience. Scholars also urged lifting the ban on the importation of books by mainland scholars, in order to legalize the lively black market in such materials that already existed.[32]

In early 1987 aging retired servicemen organized demonstrations demanding from the government the right to visit their mainland relatives before they died. Their appeal probably had a significant impact on Chiang Ching-kuo, for he had shown a special concern for retired servicemen ever since he had headed the Vocational Assistance Commission for Retired Servicemen in the 1950s. In November 1987 he made the momentous decision to permit Taiwan residents to visit their relatives on the mainland. The action demonstrated his confidence that the prosperous democratizing, free enterprise system in Taiwan would have greater appeal to all Chinese than the struggling Communist system on the mainland. Therefore, Chiang must have concluded, the risk to Taiwan's security from this bold act was tolerable.

The response in Taiwan to Chiang's decision was overwhelmingly favorable. A "mainland fever" spread across the island. By the end of 1989 at least 800,000 persons from Taiwan had visited mainland China. Two-way trade soared to $3.8 billion during 1989. The PRC established special zones and incentives for investment from Taiwan. Businessmen, who found their labor-intensive products priced out of the world market by the rapid increase in wages in Taiwan and the appreciation of the Taiwan dollar, found the low cost of labor in China attractive. Many moved their machinery to the mainland and set up operations there, particularly in the Xiamen area, where the local dialect is the same as that spoken by most Taiwanese. By the end of 1989 an estimated $1 billion had been invested by Taiwanese businessmen in enterprises on the mainland. The Tiananmen massacre in June 1989 slowed trade and travel temporarily, but it soon picked up again.

Chiang did not live to see the dramatic results of his decision to legalize travel to the China mainland, but he was given credit in both Taipei and Beijing for a wise and farsighted decision.

The Continuing Struggle for International Status

World trends during the 1980s appeared unfavorable to the ROC under Chiang Ching-kuo's leadership. Deng Xiaoping's economic opening to the outside world attracted much favorable attention from the big industrial powers. The transformation of the bipolar system into a multipolar system seemed, from Taipei's viewpoint, to weaken the anti-Communist resolve of the free world. In his address to the KMT's Central Committee in March 1986 Chiang warned:

> Our friends in the Free World should realize that current global disturbances bear a direct relationship to Communist expansionism. In particular, the Free World, misled by Communist Chinese duplicity, underestimates the long-term threat of an Asia being communized—a certain disaster for all free men.[33]

In this and other statements during the 1980s, Chiang stressed the need for self-reliance, for continuing to strengthen the ROC's economy and political system in the face of the Chinese Communist threat.

The PRC continued its relentless campaign to oust the ROC from international organizations. In 1980 it forced Taipei out of the World Bank and the International Monetary Fund. The members of Interpol and of the Asian Development Bank refused to expel the ROC representatives, but required a change of name. The ROC did not withdraw from these organizations but, during the period of Chiang's rule, declined to participate in meetings as a protest against the indignity of the name change.

The PRC was less successful in ousting the ROC from nongovernmental organizations than from intergovernmental bodies, in part because the ROC was more flexible in accepting changes of name in the former. For example, in 1981 Taipei agreed to use the designation "Chinese Taipei Olympic Committee" and a new flag and anthem in order to participate in the Olympic Games.

Despite the diplomatic isolation imposed on the ROC by Beijing, Taiwan continued its robust economic growth, after a brief slowdown in 1982 caused by the global recession. Foreign trade grew from $23.7 billion in 1978 to $110.2 billion in 1988. Foreign banks continued to open branches in Taiwan, and foreign investment flowed in. In 1979 the ROC removed its ban on direct trade with five Eastern European states. In July 1987, as part of a program to "internationalize" Taiwan's economy, individuals were authorized to export up to $5 million annually, giving strong impetus to investment abroad by Taiwan's entrepreneurs.

The ROC succeeded in substantially increasing its quasiofficial offices around the world to promote trade and cultural exchange, while the number of countries maintaining similar offices in Taiwan grew steadily. Trading nations could not afford to ignore Taiwan, which had become the 12th largest trading nation in the world. Taiwan's dynamic economy had responded during the 1980s to Chiang Ching-kuo's appeals for self-strengthening.

Conclusions

During his 16 years of stewardship from 1972 to 1988, Chiang Ching-kuo managed Taiwan's external relations with considerable success. Few observers would have predicted in 1972 that Taiwan's position in the world and vis-à-vis the China mainland would be as solid and promising as it looks today.

A review of Chiang's public statements over the period impresses the reader with the consistency—some would say rigidity—of his basic positions. His rhetoric differs little from that formulated by his father during the 1950s and 1960s, even though the free world/communist world dichotomy had changed radically by the 1970s and 1980s. The goal of reunifying China under a non-Communist system remains the same, as does the concentration on building up Taiwan as a bastion of strength for achieving that goal.

The ROC's policies under Chiang Ching-kuo's leadership, however, displayed considerable technical flexibility. Failing to gain an official relationship with the United States, the ROC adjusted to unofficial ties and became skilled at managing the relationship with its most important supporter. The ROC also showed resourcefulness in devising a wide range of unorthodox, quasiofficial methods to conduct business with its leading trading partners. Even the intransigent anti-Communist stance was eased to permit direct trade with Communist countries of Eastern Europe.

The "three no's" policy toward mainland China has been criticized as the prime example of the ROC's rigidity. Nevertheless, in legalizing indirect travel, trade, and investment, Chiang showed willingness to adjust to the reality that these activities could not be prevented. At the same time, he could portray them as conveying to the people of the mainland the Taiwan experience and thus furthering progress toward the long-term goal of unifying China under a non-Communist system. The legalization of travel, trade, and investment went part way to meet PRC demands for interchange across the Strait, creating hope in Beijing that the "three no's" might also be modified and thus easing tension between Beijing and Taipei. The tactical flexibility shown by Chiang Ching-kuo set the stage for the further flexibility displayed by his successor, Lee Teng-hui.

ENDNOTES

1. James C. H. Shen, *The U.S. and Free China: How the U.S. Sold Out Its Ally* (Washington, D.C., Aeropolis Books, Ltd., 1983), p. 51.

2. Stephen P. Gilbert and William M. Carpenter, Eds., *American and Island China: A Documentary History* (Lanham, New York, London: University Press of America, 1989), pp. 111-14.

3. Hungdah Chiu, ed. *China and the Question of Taiwan: Documents and Analysis* (New York, Washington, London: Praeger, 1973), pp. 346-48.

4. Shen, pp. 91-111.

5. Ibid., pp. 112-115.

6. *Perspectives: Selected Statements of President Chiang Ching-kuo, 1978-1983* (Taipei: Government Information Office, 1984), p. 168.

7. House Concurrent Resolution 360, 94th Cong., 1st Session, 1975.

8. Ralph N. Clough, Robert B. Oxnam, and William Watts, *The United States and China: American Perceptions and Future Alternatives* (Washington, D.C.: Potomac Associates, 1977), pp. 31-33.

9. Council for Economic Planning and Development, ROC, *Taiwan Statistical Data Book, 1989*, p. 215.

10. Ralph N. Clough, *Island China* (Cambridge, MA: Harvard University Press, 1978), p. 27.

11. Foreign Broadcast Information Service, *Daily Report, People's Republic of China* (hereafter cited as FBIS), 1 March 1973, pp. B5-B9.

12. Yung-hwan Jo., ed. *Taiwan's Future?* (Hong Kong: Union Research Institute for Arizona State University, 1974) pp. 65-70.

13. FBIS, 10 December 1974, pp. E5-E6.

14. FBIS, 25 March 1975, p. E6.

15. Hong Kong *Ta Kung Pao*, 28 February 1978, p. 3.

16. *Asahi*, 29 April 1978, p. 7.

17. FBIS, *Daily Report, Asia and Pacific* (No. 223, Supp. 42, 19 November 1973), pp. 1, 3.

18. Ibid., pp. 6,8.

19. *Taiwan Statistical Data Book, 1989*, p. 208.

20. For further details on Taiwan's substantive relations with foreign countries in the 1970s, see Ralph N. Clough, "The Republic of China and the World, 1949-1981" in Hungdah Chiu and Shao-chuan Leng, *China: Seventy Years after the Hsin Hai Revolution* (Charlottesville, Va.: University Press of Virginia, 1984), pp. 540-46.

21. Hungdah Chiu, Ed., *China and the Taiwan Issue* (New York: Praeger, 1979), pp. 252-53.

22. *Perspectives*, pp. 3,8.

23. Ibid., pp. 133-34.

24. *New York Times*, 31 December 1978; *Washington Post*, 29 December 1978.

25. Interview with Marsh Clark, Southeast Asia Bureau Chief, *Time*, 3 May 1979 (*Perspectives*, pp. 175-83).

26. Texts of 1979 and 1981 PRC statements and Premier Y. S. Sun's 1982 statement are reproduced in Robert L. Downen, *To Bridge the Taiwan Strait* (Washington, D.C.: The Council for Social and Economic Studies, Inc., 1984), pp. 104-07; 112-14; 118-23.

27. Martin L. Lasater, *The Taiwan Issue in Sino-American Strategic Relations* (Boulder, Co.: Westview Press, 1984), pp. 276-77.

28. *Perspectives*, pp. 129-30.

29. "Taiwan Agents in America and the Death of Professor Wen-chen Chen." Hearings before the Subcommittees on Asian and Pacific Affairs and Human Rights and International Organizations of the Committee of Foreign Affairs, House of Representatives, 97th Congress, 1st Session, 30 July and 6 October 1981.

30. *Perspectives*, pp. 124-25.

31. Y. S. Sun was premier from 1978 to 1984; Y. S. Tsiang was secretary-general of the KMT from 1979 to 1984; Ma Chi-chuang was secretary-general of the president's office from 1978 to 1984; Wang Sheng was director of the general political department, ministry of national defense from 1974 to 1983; and Shen Chang-huan was secretary-general of the national security council from 1979 to 1984.

32. *Shih Pao Chou K'an* (China Times Weekly) No. 108, 21-27 March, pp. 52-57 and No. 125, 18-24 July 1987, pp. 14-17.

33. *President Chiang Ching-kuo's Selected Addresses and Messages 1986* (Taipei: Government Information Office, 1987), p. 19.

CHAPTER SEVEN

The Legacy of Chiang Ching-Kuo: External Assessments Reassessed

BRIAN HOOK

INTRODUCTION

It would have taken nothing less than a particularly fertile imagination to have predicted the unfolding of international events as the last decade of the 20th century approached. Chiang Ching-kuo, who had been ailing for several years, did not physically survive to lead Taiwan in what is now seen to be a uniquely challenging period. Indeed, when his life came to an end on 13 January 1988, although with hindsight certain embryonic features of things to come were evident, the subsequent renaissance of democratic forces and the emancipation of political institutions in many parts of the world were wholly unpredictable. Even in Taiwan, where, arguably, Chiang Ching-kuo's main achievement had been taking shape, namely, to generalize a highly complicated process, the management of what for a Chinese society was an unprecedented transition from a stage of development characterized by one party *hegemony* to a new stage characterized by primary democracy, the outcome was by no means certain.

After 14 January 1988, Chiang Ching-kuo was succeeded by a new president and survived by his own legacy. The late president's testament, by focusing *inter alia* on the imperatives to oppose communism, to revive the nation, and actively to carry forward constitutional democracy without interruption, referred specifically to the transition then under way on Taiwan.[1] Similarly, many of the serious external assessments of his life dwelt on this latter issue and, by implication, suggested that ultimately the weighing of his life's work in the scales of history would depend on continuity and the successful management of this crucial transition. In the following text I reexamine a selection of the external assessments of the life of Chiang Ching-kuo made at the time of his death, in the light of continuities on Taiwan and of events throughout the world in the final years of the 1980s. My aim in reassessing them is to contribute to a more considered understanding of the nature and durability of the presidential legacy itself. In essence, the issue here is whether contemporary assessment erred, and if so, on the credit or debit side, or were incomplete, and to what extent, in the light of recent history, an adjustment is necessary.

EXTERNAL ASSESSMENTS: JANUARY 1988

Among the assessments reviewed below are selected ones made and published in Asia, the United States, and Europe at the time of Chiang Ching-kuo's death. The assessments will be addressed in those broad categories not only because of geographical propinquity and therefore the importance of shared political and economic considerations but also because, as will be shown, subsequent developments whose unfolding placed the Chiang Ching-kuo legacy in a new world environment can also be treated geographically.

On this basis the first comments to note are those from the People's Republic of China (PRC). At the party political level, the Communist party of China (CPC) Central Committee (CC) sent a message of condolence to the Kuomintang (KMT) Central Committee (CC). At the personal level, Zhao Ziyang, then general secretary of the CPC, in a speech extending condolences over the death of the "chairman of the Chinese KMT" noted that the latter had upheld a one-China policy, opposing the independence of Taiwan, standing for the reunification of China, and making "certain efforts" to relieve tension over relations between people on the two sides of the Taiwan Strait. Zhao used the occasion to reaffirm approval of the trends that emerged in the last few years of Chiang's presidency, including trade and visits by Chinese living on Taiwan to the mainland, which he viewed as a "promising momentum" that should be further built up ultimately to realize reunification. Coincidentally, the Chinese and Portuguese governments were to exchange instruments ratifying the Sino-Portuguese joint declaration on the question of Macao on 15 January 1988, an event that prompted Zhou Nan, then vice-minister of foreign affairs, to note that the successful settlements of the Hong Kong and Macao questions proved the "highly scientific nature and rationality" of the concept of "one country, two systems," a concept that he claimed would continue to exert a far-reaching impact on the cause of early reunification of Taiwan with the mainland and provide a solid foundation for the ultimate realization of that goal. Accordingly, in keeping with the temper of the times, it came as no surprise that Zhao in his speech extending condolences "hoped the new KMT leadership would size up the situation in line with the fundamental interests of the common aspirations of the Chinese people. . . ." and noted: "The people of Taiwan have a glorious patriotic tradition, long for reunification and oppose division. Together with the compatriots in Hong Kong, Macao, and overseas, they have in recent years made efforts for peaceful reunification and peace talks between the CPC and the KMT."[2]

Finally, as regards PRC reaction at the personal level to Chiang's death, the honorary chairman of the Central Committee of the Revolutionary Committee of the Chinese KMT, Qu Wu, who had once studied with the late president in the U.S.S.R., sent a telegram of condolence to the widow, Fang Liang.[3] Allowing for aspects of common political provenance, the latter gesture must also be regarded as a tactic within the broad and not unsuccessful CPC united front strategy involving Taiwan, Hong Kong, Macao, and the overseas Chinese gaining inspiration at that time from Zhao Ziyang's universally popular domestic political-economic policies. To sum up the response to Chiang's death emanating from the PRC, it is clear that the policies towards the mainland, including the relaxing of travel restrictions on certain categories of Taiwan residents (which was confidently regarded as a vehicle for the single transfer of huge sums of money to the mainland), the extraordinary growth in trade between Taiwan and the PRC through Hong Kong, the growth in Taiwanese investment both in the Pearl River delta within the outward processing arrangements of Hong Kong and across the Taiwan Strait (the latter neither formally permitted nor actively suppressed by the Taiwan administration), at the time fitted nicely into the perception of the optimum evolution of relations between CPC and the KMT.

Among the assessments made in the East Asian region, I have selected from those in Hong Kong and Japan as being of particular value and significance while noting, *en passant*, the passing of events in the Philippines since that country is of some importance as a focus of future Taiwanese investment. In the general context of what for want of a better term may be called "external China," the assessments made in Hong Kong are highly relevant. Hong Kong, we might remind ourselves, is the actual precedent being established in the application of the concept of "one country, two systems." Ironically, that concept had been developed to solve the Taiwan issue and was applied to Hong Kong first only because the United Kingdom government had for several years after 1980 urged the PRC to face up to the implications of the expiry in 1997 of the lease under whose terms a major part of the territory of the colony of Hong Kong was in the British view lawfully occupied. Hitherto, the PRC's formal position on Hong Kong held that none of the major 19th century Sino-British territorial agreements was legally binding on the grounds of their unequal nature and, as to the resolution of the issues, was encapsulated in the deliberately ambiguous but politically useful formulation that Hong Kong's future would be determined "when the time was ripe." Once the Sino-British Joint Declaration on the future of Hong Kong was signed, sealed, and delivered, informed opinion in Hong Kong knew that the fulfillment of the promise of a high degree of autonomy rested to a large extent on the PRC's perception of the likely adverse response on Taiwan (and the consequent negative effect on the prospects for reunification) of any untoward, mainland-precipitated, development in Hong Kong.

The first selected source in Hong Kong is the respected Chinese newspaper the *Ming Pao Daily News*. In an editorial on 14 January 1988 the paper drew attention to the series of reforms initiated by Chiang that had "won praise and admiration throughout the world." These the article listed as: permitting residents to go to the mainland to visit relatives, allowing opposition parties to operate openly, lifting martial law, removing restrictions on newspapers, and introducing democratic elections, all of which it stated had been unimaginable ten years earlier. The article also drew attention to the tolerance of the late president in face of the publication without hindrance of books and magazines that carried severe criticism of, and attacks on, him. It drew attention to the reforms Chiang Ching-kuo had introduced over the past one or two years and to Taiwan's continuous advance and achievement of stability and prosperity, despite pressures from "communists, other nations, and indigenous Taiwanese," concluding that, while the late president could not be compared to Chu Ko-liang of the Three Kingdoms in the later Han period in the history of China, leaders of his calibre were indeed scarce.[4]

Only the most subjective of critics could gainsay the basis for the claims made in the Ming Pao eulogy, namely Taiwan's economic and political advance under Chiang Ching-kuo's leadership. In the decade before his death, despite political problems at home and in the international arena, Taiwan displayed continued remarkable growth as the following table shows.[5]

The chief political problem domestically can be directly related to the authoritarian nature of the regime, the aspect to which Chiang Ching-kuo devoted his attention from 1986 onwards and whose worst examples aroused criticism on the international scene. Among the conspicuous excesses were the cases of Ch'en Wen-ch'eng, a professor from Carnegie Mellon University in Pittsburgh, who died in mysterious circumstances after interrogation at the Garrison Command HQ, Taipei, about alleged support of the Taiwan independence movement, and Henry Liu, a dissident journalist with U.S. citizenship, who was murdered at Daly City, California, by agents working, it was suspected, on the instructions of Taiwan security personnel. These were, in the perspective of critics of the administration, arguably like tips of a rather large

TAIWAN: TRADE FIGURES, CURRENCY RESERVES, AND PER CAPITA INCOME 1978-88

	1978	1979	1980[a]	1981	1982	1983[b]
Total Trade (USD billion)	23.7	30.8	36.6	40.3	41.1	48.3
Exports	12.7	16.1	19.8	20.7	22.2	22.8
Imports	11.0	14.7	20.3	19.6	18.9	18.2
Hard Currency Reserves	-	-	-	-	-	-
Per Capita Income (USD'000)	-	-	-	-	-	2.4

	1984[b]	1985[c]	1986	1987	1988[d]
Total Trade (USD billion)	48.3	42.2	64.0	88.6	110.2
Exports	28.1	25.5	39.8	53.6	60.6
Imports	20.2	16.7	24.2	35.0	49.6
Hard Currency Reserves	-	-	35	75	-
Per Capita Income (USD'000)	2.8	NA	3.5	4.8	5.8

[a] Approximated.
[b] 11 months.
[c] 10 months.
[d] By 1988 the NTD had been revalued and was NTD28 to the USD, having been NTD36 to the USD in 1978, weakening to NTD38 to the USD in 1981. The revaluation was in response to the U.S. current account deficit.

iceberg representing the authoritarian and potentially repressive security system, which enjoyed, apparently not without reason, an unenviable reputation, impinging on the daily lives of Taiwan citizenry.

The chief problems internationally had as their source the ever-present potential of the CPC literally to eclipse the KMT by a variety of means, were it not for the restraint imposed by the U.S.A. Since both U.S. and mainland politics were variables, the vicissitudes emanating in this context were multifarious. Suffice it to say that the ousting of Taiwan from the U.N. in 1971 initiated one trend that ushered in the systematic exclusion of Taiwan from the subordinate and associated agencies of that august body, coupled with another that severely reduced Taiwan's formal diplomatic links (as The Republic of China [ROC]), when country after country recognized the PRC. That process of "derecognition" was epitomized by the precipitate action of the U.S.A. on 1 January 1979, soon after Chiang Ching-kuo became president.[6] Even though the U.S.A. attempted to cushion the blow by passing the Taiwan Relations Act, whose subsequent negative influence on PRC-American relations is some evidence of its success in that respect, this was a serious setback for the KMT. Although the U.S.A. indicated it would be gravely concerned and would have to determine appropriate action should any effort be made to decide the future of Taiwan by other than peaceful means, listing boycotts and embargoes as matters of grave concern, the 1954 USA-ROC Mutual Defense Treaty was terminated and U.S. military sales to Taiwan were severely curtailed. Before long, as the PRC emerged from the inglorious years of the Cultural Revolution and the U.S.A. became what some would now argue to have been prematurely euphoric over the prospects for a durable and strategically important alliance with the PRC, the stage was set for the Taiwan authorities to be put under much pressure to indicate greater receptivity to mainland overtures to promote intercourse that would lead ultimately to reunification. Having regard to this concatenation of circumstances, the author of the eulogistic *Ming Pao* editorial was wholly justified in alluding to the pressures successfully withstood by Taiwan under Chiang Ching-kuo.

For a while, in the early 1980s, it did indeed appear that while Taiwan forged ahead economically, retaining the initiative in that sphere and solving the problems of people's livelihood, it could not maintain its position let alone regain the initiative in the sphere of international relations. This was in the heyday of the Deng Xiaoping-Zhao Ziyang partnership: the PRC was opening to the world, agricultural reform had produced apparently astonishing results, large numbers of Chinese were studying abroad, the cultural scene was liberalized, and unofficial trade and personal links between the mainland and Taiwan were flourishing. On Taiwan, despite the relatively rosy economic picture, stresses and strains in the political fabric became evident, the more so as seemingly well-intentioned offers by the CPC evoked a hostile response, appropriate it seemed more to the Maoist period than to the current period of the "four modernizations," and save for constant supporters, observers abroad perceived an altogether unacceptable intransigence on Taiwan's part.

The *Ming Pao* assessment, having alluded to the difficulties elaborated in the foregoing section, referred in three separate sections to the "recent reforms" initiated by Chiang Ching-kuo. The third reference is of particular significance for this current reassessment. There, it noted that people tend to become more conservative and obstinate as they grow older, adding that "the leaders of China on both sides of the strait had been able to depart from this rule by, despite their advancing years, upholding reform and opening to the outside world." It is now clear that while this assessment remained true for Taiwan (and, up to the time of writing, the reform process initiated by Chiang Ching-kuo has *mutatis mutandis* continued), that across the strait a crisis occurred just over a year after this statement was published, culminating in a reassertion of the rule from which the mainland leadership had seemingly departed. Although the crisis that brought the violent suppression of the democracy movement, the ousting of Zhao Ziyang and his advisers, the curtailing of the modernization program, and systematic political rectification was surmounted in the short term, clearly its legacy will not readily be forgotten. The fact that in the final analysis, the assumption in the *Ming Pao Daily News* editorial proved unfounded, requires some explanation. The crucial issue appears, with hindsight, to have been the ability of Chiang Ching-kuo to isolate those KMT leaders likely to espouse conservatism regarding the further development of Taiwan's politics while persuading those who remained doubtful of the need for urgent reforms.[7]

Reference has been made above to the inauspicious events and, for Taiwan, adverse trends in international relations to which the *Ming Pao* editorials also alluded. A better understanding of the challenge facing Chiang Ching-kuo and his response to it can be had by taking fully into account both the international and internal situations. By the early 1980s, internally Taiwan had already become a comparatively well-integrated society. Friction between mainlanders and Taiwanese, a perennial problem of earlier decades, had been significantly reduced by the greater opportunities for material advancement in a modernizing, wealth-creating society. However, political participation had remained at a low level wholly inconsistent with the advance of the Taiwan economy and the maturity of its citizens. With the benefit of hindsight, it is evident that this state of affairs in which political participation was severely circumscribed could not survive for much longer; two trends had been established to promote change. One trend was the impact of generational change as younger men, educated abroad, orientated toward Taiwan, rather than the mainland, but with a cosmopolitan outlook, began to take over from the first-generation, conservative KMT officials. The second trend was the presence of a small but growing non-KMT political movement based on representatives of the emerging well-educated, successful middle-class on Taiwan. The members of this movement, usually referred to in the literature as Tangwai or extra-party (on the sense of extra-mural), lacked cohesion but enjoyed considerable support as was evident on the occasions when they contested elections.

Chiang Ching-kuo responded to these trends and to the dangers inherent in the loss of initiative in the international arena by launching the reforms for which he is rightly given credit in the *Ming Pao* editorial. However, while there remained no potential impediment in his lifetime, such was his charisma and authority, there was growing concern about the succession. In this context, both the Taiwanese and the mainland leaders faced certain issues in common. Both were old, both charismatic, and neither had an absolutely free hand to determine the succession in that ultimate power was vested in the military if it chose to act. However, Chiang remained adamant that should he die in office, his successor, as required by the constitution, would be Vice President Lee Teng-hui, and not another member of his family, such as his half-brother Chiang Wei-kuo, secretary-general of the National Security Conference, or his son, Hsiao-wu, or Wang Sheng, who until his translation to Paraguay as ambassador had appeared to be a contender. By skillfully neutralizing those forces that might inhibit reform, Chiang showed his long-term commitment to it. Moreover, the commitment appears to have been to an ongoing process rather than a single act or acts of reform. This appears to distinguish Chiang Ching-kuo from Deng Xiaoping since the latter, from his accession to power, established a pattern of reform characterized by the exercise of state power to retard advances that appeared to lead to systemic change, the most recent exercise of which has created doubts as to the viability of existing reforms.

Chiang Ching-kuo's commitment to reform was never more evident than in 1986. To what extent any one of the trends or set of circumstances already described was responsible is difficult to establish. It may be that, although the societies, governments, and economies of Taiwan and the Philippines are not remotely comparable, the existence of conspicuous contradictions in both societies convinced Chiang Ching-kuo that the rapid overthrow of the Marcos regime was ominous and that this indeed became a catalyst for the initiatives that followed on Taiwan. By the end of the year, an as yet not lawfully established political party was contesting elections to the National Assembly and to the Legislative Yuan, while the president established a commission to consider what were called the "four sensitive issues": establishing new political parties, lifting martial law, electing the provincial governor, and superannuating the aging mainlanders in the National Assembly, Legislative, and Control Yuans. Thus, at a stroke, having weighed all the issues, Chiang Ching-kuo launched Taiwan into a major transition, the results of which were so highly commended in the *Ming Pao Daily News* assessment of his life.

A second major selected appraisal of Chiang Ching-kuo published in Hong Kong is that which appeared in the *Far Eastern Economic Review* (*FEER*). Although not notably based on economic analysis (the only specific evidence in this regard to be adduced drew attention to the speed with which the Taiwan stock market rebounded from the fall following the announcement of the president's death, which was seen as a mark of progress and maturity and economic robustness achieved during the nine years of his presidency), the *FEER* appraisal highlighted the range of experience of Chiang Ching-kuo and also his personal qualities. The implication of this approach is that because of his rich experience, encompassing a period as a revolutionary youth with Trotskyist leanings, another as a common laborer in factories and on farms during the decade spent in the U.S.S.R., another as director of the KMT military's general political department, and yet another as organizer of the China Youth Corps before he became minister of defense, vice premier and premier and then president, only Chiang Ching-kuo had the political capacity to succeed in the initiative launched between 1986 and his death. Accordingly, his successor would not find it at all easy to take the reform further.[8]

Besides drawing attention to the link between experience and political capacity, the *FEER* also made important points about Chiang Ching-kuo's personal qualities. In particular, it referred to his steadfastness and courage during the last year of his life when the reforms he had initiated were at a most delicate stage and he had to contend with a worsening physical incapacity. Consequently the image of a very popular president formed from his demonstrated affection for the working population (a quality never actually in evidence in his rather aloof father) was further enhanced as he fought tenaciously to fulfill public engagements when the physical ordeal was at its worst. By doing so, he had signaled his hold on power and the longer that was the case, the greater the scope and prospect for the durability of the reforms. The *FEER* appraisal drew attention in particular to the example of 25 December 1987, when he appeared in a wheelchair on the occasion of the Constitution Day ceremony, and his speech was read for him, as being of crucial significance not just for upholding his authority but for keeping the opposition challenge at bay. In retrospect, that final public appearance, while testifying to his strength of character and dedication, it is claimed was also the occasion that beyond doubt had implicitly vindicated his reform policies since there was an unprecedented display of dissent both inside and outside the Chungshan Memorial Hall. After that event none could seriously question the case for reform or the steps initiated by him. When it reported the news of his death less than a month later, it is significant that the Taiwan press had abandoned the traditional contrived court language used at the time of Chiang Kai-shek's death, and instead opted for coverage more in keeping with the progress and modernity of Taiwan, the confidence and maturity of its citizens, and the evolution of the KMT into a modernized political party. By focusing on recollections of his populist contacts, the media illustrated unique personal qualities which obviously had endeared him to wide sections of the population and even won him the respect of Kang Ning-hsiang, the leader of the Democratic Progressive party, both a long-standing adversary and a main beneficiary of his reform program, who referred to his death as a "great loss" and who, out of respect for him, suspended DPP political activities for a month.

Together with the PRC and Hong Kong, the other source of selected comment in the region is Japan. The Japanese response has, however, to be viewed in a different context. For one thing, Taiwan was formerly administered as part of the Japanese empire while Chiang Ching-kuo was the son of a leader whose life had been devoted to the liberation of China from imperialist influence, and was himself a patriot whose career was in a similar mould. At the same time, Japan, once again a world power, under the aegis and at the expense of the U.S.A., emerged from defeat to assume by economic means the role formerly sought by military might, in East and Southeast Asia. Conscious of this position, which now included a beneficial and potentially lucrative role in the modernization of a China inspired by the Zhao-Deng reform program, encompassing interests in Taiwan and Hong Kong, Japan would be expected to be correct and circumspect in its reaction to Chiang Ching-kuo's death.

In the event, there is little to choose in terms of content between the two selected Japanese commentaries, both published on 14 January 1988, one appearing in the Tokyo-based *Yomiuri*

Shimbun, a conservative source, the other in the Osaka-based *Asahi Shimbun*, a left-of-centre source. The *Yomiuri Shimbun* provided more details of Chiang Ching-kuo's career, referring to his being the first son of Chiang Kai-shek, to the period 1925-1937, during the United Front, spent in the U.S.S.R., to his marriage to a Russian woman (Sofanina: Jiang Fang-liang), focusing on details of his political work in the Ministry of Defense prior to becoming minister, and to the period as premier then secretary-general of the Central Committee of the KMT and president. It credits Chiang Ching-kuo with having led Taiwan to the status of a NIC despite the vicissitudes of derecognition by the U.S.A. and Japan, followed by the current period of diplomatic isolation. It noted that in 1986, responding to the demands of Taiwanese for more democracy and to pressure from within, he was responsible for a change in the political direction of Taiwan. This, it implied, released pressure and averted an explosion of discontent, showing Chiang to be a realist.

The particular policies to which *Yomiuri Shimbun* referred were his conceding to the principle of opposition parties, the lifting of martial law, and the authorizing of travel to the mainland to visit relatives. Regarding the future, *Yomiuri Shimbun* said his death raised the question as to whether these policies would survive. It quoted Premier Yu Kuo-hua as stating that the loss of the president was great and the most complex task of recovering the mainland remained. This had invited the inference that while the late president's own emphasis had shifted to the democratization of Taiwan, implicitly acknowledging the "permanence" of the status quo as a compromise with the forces advocating self-determination, the less reform-minded and more conservative premier's strategic focus had remained on the mainland and the conditions for reunification.[9]

The *Asahi Shimbun* in its coverage also drew attention to the role of Yu Kuo-hua, indicating that, while Lee Teng-hui would constitutionally succeed Chiang, a new era had begun and Taiwan would not in future be ruled by one person since the president and premier would both be central figures. The *Asahi Shimbun's* analysis of the reforms carried out under the late president differed in emphasis from that of *Yomiuri*, inviting the perception that Chiang's contributions toward diluting the militarism of the KMT and promoting further economic development had enabled Taiwan to achieve the status of a NIC. It also stated that Chiang had tried to reconcile Taiwan to its isolation, permitting mainlanders to visit their native places, and innovatingly responding to pressures for democratization by sanctioning political pluralism. The *Asahi Shimbun* also drew attention to the succession by Lee Teng-hui, the significance of which was seen as giving emphasis to domestic politics. This, together with the possibility of greater power being enjoyed in future by opposition parties, was not viewed as reducing the chances of reunification with the mainland, moves towards which might, the *Asahi Shimbun* claimed, be given impetus by the president's death. In keeping with the special interests of Japan, which as already noted extend to internal and external China, the paper also drew attention to the response in the PRC to the death of Chiang Ching-kuo, noting that a main TV news program had been interrupted to record the suspension by Taiwan TV of its normal programs on the announcement of the event. This, it claimed, was an unusual response indicating the importance attached to the event by the PRC authorities.[10]

Next to the regional assessments of Chiang Ching-kuo, those made in the U.S.A. are most important, and I have selected for consideration the extensive coverage offered by the *New York Times*. One would expect this newspaper to view the significance of his passing both in the context of Sino-U.S. relations and in the related context of the future of Taiwan itself. The State Department's view, expressed by spokesman Charles E. Redman, was clearly aimed at avoiding any problems with the PRC and said simply: "We note with great sadness the passing of this respected leader." Quoting William H. Gleysteen, Jr., a China specialist and former career diplomat who had served in the posts of deputy in the U.S. Embassy to the ROC and ambassador to South Korea, the *New York Times* stated: "Many people thought he would be a mediocre leader, but he turned out to be a very fine one understanding that whatever the formal slogans might be the reality was that the government was on Taiwan and was not likely to be leaving soon." Ambassador Gleysteen was also quoted as attributing Chiang Ching-kuo the initiation of active, genuine political liberalization on the island. Quoting the director of the China Council of the Asia Society, Anthony J. Kane, the paper stated that "it is clear that Chiang Ching-kuo was a very strong leader," adding "the challenge now to his successor and to the ruling party, the KMT is to maintain the momentum that has been established towards modernization." Regarding the future of the trends he had established, the paper's assessment quoted Alan D. Romberg, a China specialist and former State Department official, currently senior fellow for Asia at the Council on Foreign Relations: "He took steps to ensure there would not be a family dynasty or a military regime that followed him recognizing that either of those things would set back the objectives that he was working for."

The *NYT* assessment, which set the scene for comment the following day (as did the *Hong Kong Ming Pao Daily News*) on the succession by Lee Teng-hui, could be summed up as an elaboration of the points made in these quotations. However, it drew attention to the late president's having taken over from his father a Taiwan that, since the thrust of policy was to recover the mainland, was a fortress in which there were severe tensions between the mainland and native communities; it also drew attention to his early resolve as prime minister to increase public support for the government, which had long been authoritarian and repressive. Accordingly, he had begun to cut a more benign public figure, wearing a turtleneck sweater and a wind cheater during tours of the countryside, and making unannounced visits to listen to complaints by farmers and villagers about bureaucracy and other problems. He had also confronted such problems as corruption, poor transport, and endemic poverty. The *NYT* quoted an unidentified attorney in Taiwan as having said in 1975 that the government in the previous two or three years had finally realized its survival depended on the development of Taiwan. Regarding his political work the *NYT* drew attention to the achievements as president in bringing Taiwanese into the island's political administrative and military spheres, noting that about 70 percent of the KMT membership and the great majority of those in the military rank-and-file were native Taiwanese. It noted further the formation, though not yet as a legal entity, of the Democratic Progressive Party (DPP), in the period when he oversaw the opening of the political system of Taiwan.[11]

To assess the European view of Chiang Ching-kuo I have selected British, French, German, Swiss, and Spanish sources and researched, to little avail, several Soviet Russian sources. The *London Times* published a full length obituary on 14 January 1988 with the subtitle "President of a prosperous Taiwan." The significant feature of this article is that while it draws attention to the commitment of its subject to Taiwan's "economic miracle," including his advocacy of high technology and support for the export-orientated policies of technocratic advisers, to his firmly anticommunist conviction, including maintaining the claim to sovereignty over the mainland, and to his relaxing some of his father's policies and subsequently revealing "a disposition to reform," on balance, the assessment gives a less sympathetic view of the late president than any other so far examined. There is no attempt at gainsaying the fact that Chiang Ching-kuo presided over an ever more prosperous and latterly a more democratic Taiwan, though no mention is made of the ultimate toleration of pluralism. It traces his life from his birth in Fenghua, through his education at Sun Yat-sen University in Moscow ("then his father's ally") where having been accused of "trouble making" he was cleared by Zhou En-lai, through the remainder of the period in the U.S.S.R., when "after graduating he was held almost as a hostage working in a factory, on a farm, and in a gold mine" before meeting and marrying the Russian woman who had nursed him through a serious illness. Noting that he returned to China in 1937, fluent in Russian and a convinced anticommunist, the article recounts his systematic progression through the hierarchy, indicating that from the 1950s he was the effective master of the security police, the secret services, and the political commissars in the army. Moreover, as the Generalissimo spent more time in seclusion, the young Chiang consolidated a formidable power base in the government, party, and army. According to the anonymous author: "In the course of this, he won a reputation for sharp temper and ruthlessness." Dr. Wu Kuo-chen, respected governor of Taiwan province, 1949-53, accused him of having "no understanding whatsoever of modern democratic government," attributing his authoritarianism to his Russian training. The obituary continues: "Chiang himself boasted of having broken up more than 500 separate communist conspiracies over a three- to four-year period, as a result of which some 2,500 people were probably executed." The obituary did, however, note that in 1948, when relinquishing the post of deputy economic adviser in Shanghai after having failed to stem the rampant inflation, profiteering and black-marketeering in the months before the CPC take-over, he publicly apologized to the people for not having done a better job. Nonetheless, the basically unsympathetic tenor of this assessment established in the second paragraph is maintained throughout: "He is remembered as a tough politician-administrator—manipulative, bullying and cajoling—who also had the good fortune to preside over an economic miracle that owed as much to the intrinsic vitality of the people as to their political leadership."[12]

Among the continental European assessments of Chiang Ching-kuo, the most comprehensive were found in French and German sources such as the center-left newspaper, *Le Monde*, the right-wing paper *Le Figaro*, the right-of-center journal *Der Spiegel*, and center paper *Die Zeit*. References were also found in the left-wing French paper *Liberation* and the communist paper *L'Humanite*. Besides French and German sources, the prestigious Swiss paper *Neue Zurcher Zeitung* carried a long obituary notice. Significantly, in view of Chiang Ching-kuo's past record of over a decade spent in Stalinist U.S.S.R., during which time he is said to have deemed his father a "traitor" to the cause for his sanctioning the 1917 Shanghai massacre of communists, temporarily to have espoused Trotskyist politics, and to have been detained unwillingly, none of the main Soviet press organs published an obituary. In the leading organs—*Pravda, Izvestiya, Literaturnaya Gazeta* and *Moscow News*—the only reference found was in *Pravda* on 20 January 1988, a week after Chiang Ching-kuo's death, which quoted a Tass source about the succession of Lee Teng-hui "according to the laws of Taiwan."[13]

Among the points made in *Le Monde* were that Chiang Ching-kuo had been a pragmatic ruler, and that only he could have succeeded in imposing the framework within which the current evolution of Taiwan politics had taken place. By contrast, it was considered that Lee Teng-hui would have to come to terms with the KMT military. However, while the evolution was not expected to be interrupted, since it was supported by the people of Taiwan, any attempts by radicals to promote independence would be viewed from Beijing as a *casus belli*. With the possibility that any trouble over the succession would precipitate an economic crisis and in turn a political crisis, thus increasing the possibility of interference from the mainland, the paper anticipated a smooth, calm transition. It noted that despite derecognition the U.S.A. remained a major bilateral trading partner and supplier of defensive weapons, much to the displeasure of the PRC, and that "the American people would be represented at the funeral of their wise and old friend." Another article in *Le Monde* referred to the late president as a "prudent reformer." It referred to his prolonged stay in the U.S.S.R. "partly as a student partly as a hostage" where he had gained his knowledge of totalitarian systems, and also to his experience in China before 1949 when he had failed to get an orderly devaluation of the Chinese dollar. In the sections dealing with the post-1975 period, the article claimed that he had foiled an attempt by his stepmother, Song Mei-ling, to determine the succession (a fait echoner une tentative de sa belle-mere . . . de s'emposer de la succession). Thereafter he had prudently launched a reform program that "pleased neither the old guard nor the military," the former committed to the reconquest and the latter preoccupied with security. Step by step, it claimed, he had moved his "pawns," liberated political prisoners, and placed Taiwanese in responsible positions to the disadvantage of those from the mainland. Accordingly, Lee Teng-hui had become his constitutional successor in 1984. The article concluded that Chiang Ching-kuo would be seen as having "transformed the island refuge into a shop-window of capitalist prosperity, one of the Asian tigers."[14]

In the article published in *Le Figaro*, also on 14 January 1988, the author, Francois Nivolon, focused more closely on the late president's earlier years. Entitled "La fin d'une dynastie," the article drew attention to Chiang Ching-kuo's having been refused permission to return to China first in April 1927 and again in 1930, being sent by the Soviet authorities to work successively in the electrical industry, on a farm, and as a technician in a gold mine before being sent in 1933 to a consumer goods factory in Sverdlovsk in the Urals, where he met and, in March 1935, married his wife, who was a Russian orphan. The author noted that his return to China was eventually authorized by Stalin in 1937, by which time he had perfect Russian, adding that this did not help when, in 1945, his father sent him on a mission to the U.S.S.R. where he stayed for a month and met both Stalin and Molotov.[15]

As for the other French sources cited, the Catholic paper *La Croix* on the same day referred to him as "anticommuniste reformateur" and declared the end of a dynasty which had failed on the mainland but brought prosperity to Taiwan. The left-wing *Liberation*, in a specially commissioned long article by Dominik Barouch published on 14 January 1988 entitled "Mort du dernier de la dynastie des Chiang Kai-shek," surveyed his life and work, referred to his announcement in 1986 that there would "not be a dynasty," and dubbed him an "anticommuniste convaincu" who had maintained the policy of "three no's" while rejecting, equally, the calls for a unilateral proclamation of Taiwan's independence. The paper reported the view that his death would set back any PRC plan for reunification and reinforce the challenge from the DPP.[16] The communist paper *L'Humanite* on the same day, in a significantly short report covering his illness and his succeeding Chiang Kai-shek, concluded that had it not been for American protection the KMT forces would not have secured their island refuge.[17]

In Germany, on 18 January 1988, *Der Spiegel* published a short factual account of the late president's life and work, noting that he had been a communist aspirant himself for a while, as a result of education in the U.S.S.R. and working in "Stalin's empire" until 1937, before becoming a radical scourge of the communists, "Kommunistenfresser."[18] A more comprehensive and analytical article was published in *Die Zeit* on 22 January, entitled "Taiwan: the end of a dynasty," in which the assessment of Chiang Ching-kuo was that although he had countered the Deng Xiaoping formula of "one country-two systems" with "the three no's," he himself had chipped the first stones out of "the wall of hatred" the communists and nationalists had erected by permitting humanitarian visits to relatives in the PRC. In fact, the paper argued, this was a signal for a cautious opening towards Peking. Noting the KMT's substituting the "signal-fire effect" of the economic miracle for military power in the promotion of a model for the emancipation of China from its "calcified and encrusted command economy" and the loosening of the political reins by the authoritarian regime in Taiwan, the article stated that Chiang Ching-kuo must have known his time was limited. It continued: "He was the only politician with sufficient authority to compel resisting KMT officials to follow the path of internal liberalization." It suggested that Lee Teng-hui would be a "transitional president" since he lacked a power base of his own. In a final paragraph whose inaccurate prediction is a tribute to the careful initiatives launched by Chiang Ching-kuo, the article reads "As in Peking, however, the hesitant reforms will probably be difficult to undo. On both sides of the Strait of Formosa, the old images of enmity are beginning to pale. Younger, pragmatic politicians are replacing the veterans of the Civil War. The signs point to rapprochement through change between the two Chinas."[19]

Finally, the main Spanish newspaper *El Pais*, in a lengthy article based on agency reports from Taipei and Madrid and published on 14 January 1988, also placed the death of Chiang Ching-kuo in the context of relations with the PRC, after having noted that from 1975 the late president had begun to give a new openness to Taiwan politics through the renewal of the KMT and reducing the power of the National Security Council, and to include more Taiwanese in the ranks of the directorate of the KMT to retard aspirations for independence and self-determination. These policies culminated in the adoption of a more relaxed policy towards the mainland, whose leaders were also worried by the support for self-determination at a time when the agreements about the future of Hong Kong and Macao gave reason to look toward the reunification of China.[20]

CONCLUSION

The aim of this paper has been to examine assessments of the late president, Chiang Ching-kuo, made at the time of his death, and to ascertain in the light of events to what extent they were accurate. Looking back over the evidence, one strand running throughout is of a successful reformer who had the necessary combination of status, experience, charisma, humanity, and, insofar as one can gather, freedom from the moral turpitude that erodes the prestige of so many modern leaders, to convince conservative members of the case for reform. There was nobody else alive, certainly not in the KMT, who approached his range and level of experience, gained, as we have seen, first in testing times in the U.S.S.R., then in Nationalist China, and latterly on Taiwan. As a result of the enforced stay in the U.S.S.R., he appears to have matured from impressionistic youthfulness to understanding of the functioning of a totalitarian system with all that implies, and to have become a convinced anticommunist ("anticommuniste convaincu" and "anticommuniste reformateur"). This contributed to his stance in the 1970s and 1980s but before that to the role of "Kommunistenfresser."[21] While contributing to his struggle against the CPC, this understanding clearly also assisted him in his ability to thwart perceived subversive forces from all directions when he headed Taiwan's security apparatus and also later when, following the politically embarrassing assassination of Henry Liu, a U.S. citizen on U.S. soil, he had to deal severely with members of his own administration.

A further enrichment of his experience clearly occurred during the debacle of the final years of the Civil War. The psychological impact of such experience cannot be overestimated. In Europe, since the Second World War, Germany has pursued a policy of sound money above all else, for fear of a repetition of the hyperinflation of the prewar period. By contrast, Britain has, until recently, been preoccupied with job preservation at the expense of competitiveness in the context of a pervasive postimperial syndrome (the false belief that "British is best" lingered for decades after the loss of captive colonial markets). For Chiang Ching-kuo, economic prudence and planning were other imperatives, and this was never more evident than when he was a key figure in promoting first, the ten basic economic development projects in the 1970s, and then the 12 major new projects in the 1980s, while also ensuring that Taiwan had the educated and trained personnel to run the economy. In combination, these measures saw Taiwan through the oil shocks, and by virtue of the ability to export competitively, the shock of derecognition and diplomatic isolation.

Lastly, as regards experience, although not a well-traveled statesman, he had observed the need for the regular renewal of political parties, not least because of the peculiar position of the KMT on Taiwan, and for the citizenry freely to identify with the ruling party. To this end, unlike his predecessor, he strove to achieve a practical balance in the leadership circles and rank and file of the party between the ever-present but slowly fading historical aspirations for military reconquest and the emerging, dynamic, contemporary reality of Taiwan's significance as a potential model for the evolution of the system on the mainland. It was perhaps of particular significance that at the fourth plenum of the 11th Central Committee and the 11th Central Advisory Committee of the KMT on 10 December 1979, at a difficult political conjuncture, referring to the mainland, he spoke of making a *political* landing based on the experience gained in developing Taiwan.

Clearly, the assessments made of Chiang Ching-kuo were on the whole accurate. However, given events since 1988, what adjustments would informed opinion make if such assessments were being revised for imminent publication? In retrospect, one point raised in the *Ming Pao Daily News* is particularly poignant: that it was fortunate that both of China's aged leaders, the late Chiang Ching-kuo and Deng Xiaoping, were committed to reform, and that both were exceptions to the rule that the older a Chinese leader was, the more conservative he became. In the event, the world has witnessed the limits to reform on the mainland under the CPC while, so far, the process initiated in Taiwan by the late president has continued to evolve. Even if in future there were to be a successful challenge within the constitution from, for example, a member of the Chiang family, provided the process were lawful and given the existing stage of social and political development, in certain respects it would now be more analogous to a member of the Lee Kuan-yew family seeking election in Singapore than the contravention of a solemn pledge made by the late president.[22] It appears that the essential difference to be noted is that between the perception of a Leninist CPC informed by Marxist ideology, on the one hand, and that of a "Leninist" KMT informed by the political principles enunciated by Sun Yat-sen, as modernized through links with the capitalist economies of such political democracies as the U.S.A., on the other.

In this general context, the relative durability of the reform under Chiang Ching-kuo is a reflection of his application of party precepts. The KMT, for a very long period a skillful exponent of martial law that inhibited the development of constitutional democracy, had remained ultimately committed to such an eventuality by virtue of its role as a moral and technical vanguard responding to its Chinese traditions. By contrast, although the CPC fostered far-reaching economic reforms in the heyday of the Deng-Zhao partnership, at several crucial junctures in the decade after 1978 it either retarded or halted the trends towards reform, as liberalization challenged that party's tradition. Ultimately the CPC, two years after the KMT lifted martial law and invoked reform, imposed martial law to crush what it by then had identified as an antiparty rebellion. Thus, in revising the assessments it would be necessary to emphasize what appears to be the durability of the reforms that may be attributed to Chiang Ching-kuo, so long as Taiwan remains free to manufacture and trade, and the people's livelihood continues to improve. In this context it does appear that while the economic performance of Taiwan under Chiang Ching-kuo's leadership is exemplary, he himself intuited and applied the principles on which the functional theory of democratic transitions is based, namely, that in the longer run the democratization of the political institutions of an hitherto authoritarian regime, rather than weakening it, actually enhances its legitimacy and appeal. Thus, the legalizing of the DPP and its contesting elections are likely to strengthen the position of the KMT and contribute to its enjoying a position in Taiwan's politics analogous to that of the Liberal Democratic party in Japan. If this is so, it would be appropriate to give credit where it is due in the assessment of Chiang Ching-kuo.

Had the CPC been able to continue with its reforms, having regard to the temper of the times, not only would the prospects for an evolving *modus vivendi* between the KMT and, *ipso facto*, an institutionally democratized CPC arguably have been rosier, but the future implementing of the principle of "one country-two systems" might have been less fraught with uncertainty. Accordingly, a further and arguably a historically more significant adjustment to be made in the assessments of Chiang Ching-kuo is that in responding to the multifarious pressures on Taiwan he oversaw the adoption of politics that, had reforms in the PRC continued and its institutions become democratized, prepared Taiwan both to launch and to respond to initiatives that could have ushered in a new and symbiotic relationship with the mainland. The development of such a relationship, with all that it implies for the region, including the future of Hong Kong, is for the time being suspended. When it is resumed, as it certainly will be, the full extent of the reforms initiated during the Chiang Ching-kuo presidency will become apparent as will be their role in the modernization of China.

ENDNOTES

1. An official translation into English of Chiang Ching-kuo's will appeared in *Free China Review* (supplement) of February 1988. The will, dated 5 January 1988, exhorts the government and the people to promote constitutional democracy without interruption. Lee Teng-hui in his swearing in speech on 13 January and Ma Ying-jeou, the KMT spokesman, on 15 January, both acknowledged these aims.

2. *Beijing Review*, 25-31 January 1988, pp. 5-6. See also *The South China Morning Post*, Hong Kong, 15 January 1988, and the *New York Times*, "Beijing Extols Taiwan's Chief on his Death," 15 January 1988.

3. *Beijing Review, loc. cit.*

4. *Ming Pao Daily News*, Hong Kong, 14 and 15 January 1988.

5. Statistics drawn from *Quarterly National Economic Trends*, Taiwan Area, ROC, published in Taipei by the Directorate General of the Budget, Accounts and Statistics of the Executive Yuan, May 1990, supplemented by information released by government sources and published in the *Free China Journal*, 1978-88.

6. When Chiang Ching-kuo became president he took much of the policy-making power with him, having been well schooled: firstly, as deputy premier from 1969 (by which time his position within the military had been consolidated) and chairman of the Financial and Economic Committee; secondly, from 1972 as premier, when, by restoring constitutional power to the economic and financial ministries that had hitherto been enjoyed by an extraconstitutional body, the Economic Planning Agency, he gained their support; thirdly, throughout this

process he had been supported as premier, vice president, and president by Yen Chia-kan, who was able in both political and economic affairs.

7. Although there have been internal challenges in a changed domestic and international environment since 1988, the election of Lee Teng-hui, the convening of the National Affairs Conference, and its outcome indicate that the reformist trend, although retarded, is firmly established.

8. *Far Eastern Economic Review*, Hong Kong, 26 January 1988.

9. *Yomiuri Shimbun*, Tokyo, 14 January 1988.

10. *Asahi Shimbun*, Tokyo, 14 January 1988.

11. *New York Times*, 14 and 15 January 1988.

12. "Mr. Chiang Ching-kuo President of a Prosperous Taiwan," *The Times*, London, 14 January 1988. Of all the material surveyed for this paper, this obituary was unique in its criticism of the career of its subject. It is unsigned and its provenance is unclear; it has not been possible to identify the author. It is conceivable that the obituary was prepared a decade or so earlier and updated thereafter so that the main achievements of the presidency were overshadowed by events when Taiwan was less secure and its governance less liberal.

13. *Pravda*, Moscow, 20 January 1988, quoting a Tass report of 19 January 1988.

14. *Le Monde*, Paris, 14 January 1988; "La liberalisation de la 'petite Chine' ne semble pas remise en cause"; "Tchiang Ching-kuo un reformateur prudent," ibid., 15 January 1988.

15. "La fin d'une dynastie," *Le Figaro*, Paris, 14 January 1988.

16. "La mort du president taiwanais Chiang Ching-kuo," *La Croix*, Paris, 15 January 1988; "Mort du denier de la dynastie des Chiang Kai-shek," *Liberation*, Paris, 14 January 1988.

17. "Mort du chef du regime de Taiwan," *L'Humanite*, Paris, 14 January 1988.

18. *Der Spiegel*, Hamburg, 18 January 1988.

19. *Die Zeit*, Hamburg, 22 January 1988.

20. *El Pais*, Madrid, 14 and 15 January 1988.

21. See footnotes 15, 16, and 18.

22. The incipient challenge to Lee Teng-hui and the secretary-general of the president's office, Li Yuan-zu, by the president of the Judicial Yuan, Lin Yang-kang, and the secretary-general of the National Security Council, Chiang Wego, a son of Chiang Kai-shek, was constitutional and it was resolved constitutionally.

CHAPTER EIGHT

Reflections on Leadership, China, and Chiang Ching-kuo

ROBERT A. SCALAPINO

Defined simply, leadership is the capacity, individually or collectively, to influence, shape, or control decisions and actions affecting others. It derives from a variety of capacities, including the ability to coerce; superior intellect, knowledge, or experience; the requisite personality to persuade; or those personal antecedents and connections that provide automatic legitimacy. Most of these qualities are to some degree culture-related in the precise forms they take. In their relative weight, they also bear a strong relationship to a society's stage of development.

What are the principal tasks of leadership and the standards whereby the quality of leaders is measured? First, authority or legitimacy must be obtained and maintained by some combination of the attributes outlined above. Even the most ruthless individual cannot exercise power over others by coercion alone, at least for any protracted period of time. And without the sanction of those governed, the ruler's reach is constricted in a myriad of ways.

At an early point, moreover, valid priorities must be established, with goals attuned to both the needs and capacities of the society. Then, an organizational structure and the personnel capable of achieving those priorities must be constructed. The caliber of leadership is often best revealed by the type of individuals recruited for the critical tasks at hand, and the ability of leader to delegate decision making to them when appropriate.

Utilizing a variety of appeals, the effective leader must also be able to persuade a sizable number of the citizenry to accept the policies proffered. In this connection, appeals both to self-interest and to a broader set of values (an ideology) as well as a communal commitment (nationalism) must be employed.

Another test of effective leadership is the capacity to select the proper and, if possible, the optimal timing for action. Either "prematurism" or "tailism" exacts its price.

Finally, and by no means less important, successful leaders must be receptive to change when circumstances dictate a new course. Not a few leaders—especially those long in power—lose their authority when they become ossified in positions rendered passé by developments.

One should note the changing requirements of leadership in the course of social evolution. Among primitive mankind, physical strength commanded greatest respect. Even then, however, there must have been some premium upon intellect, or perhaps the appropriate term would be "cunning." As societies evolved, moreover, those who had accumulated experience were valued more highly—hence, the homage paid to elders. Nor can one neglect the dominant values to which a given people adhered as their culture evolved. The mystical, the sacred, became a source of the legitimization of authority at a very early point in mankind's sociopolitical evolution.

What is important to the student of our times, however, is the fact that certain secular ideologies could play a similar role. Hybrid political-religious creeds have also flourished in this century. This is one of the reasons why the idea of many earlier theorists, including Max Weber, that a routinized bureaucracy would supplant charismatic leadership has proven only partially correct at most. The growing complexity of modern governance has bred a special class of technocrats. It is true that institutions firmly implanted have placed restraints on leaders. Even the traditional monarchical institution did so in many settings, among them China. Yet in our times, we have seen countless examples of leaders who overrode the institutions under which they supposedly operated and the technocrats to whom they were supposedly beholden, appealing to a "higher faith," in the process causing their subjects to equate their person with that faith. Thus, charisma has lived on.

We have witnessed that phenomenon most powerfully in this century via two channels. One is the resurgence of religious fundamentalism, especially fundamentalist Islam. No one will forget the visage of the Ayatollah Khomeini and the degree to which he was able to mobilize his people through a mixture of religion, nationalism, and xenophobia. It is a similar force that worries the Russians today as they contemplate the rise of Central Asian nationalism, a movement that could easily spill over into other nations. But Islam does not stand alone in the realm of politicized religion. Witness the march of militant Hinduism in India. And in the realm of Christianity, who can forget the saga of Jonestown or the activities of the Reverend Sun Myung Moon and his followers?

In this age of extraordinarily rapid changes, many individuals need some type of faith to prevent their moorings from being swept away. If secular authorities fall short in providing values, the need will be filled by others. The reemergence of religion in the forefront of politics in various settings testifies to this fact—a fact overlooked by virtually all social scientists until recently.

Yet there has been one type of secular cause that seemed to provide sureness of faith required to supplant religion or other competitors. I refer to Marxism-Leninism. Marxism-Leninism promised utopia, and in this sense, salvation. In contrast to liberalism, it was based on the ultimate perfectibility of mankind. Moreover, in its institutional structure as well as its ideology, it encompassed the avant-garde words and phrases of the 20th century: democracy, people's government, a classless society, and ultimately the brotherhood of man.

How could a Stalin, a Mao, a Kim Il-sung, and a Castro evolve out of such a set of promises? One important factor, of course, is that Leninism was born and evolved generally in economically backward societies, lacking a critical mass of literate, politically aware citizens. The traditions were often monarchical or, in any case, those of autocracy. When the institutional restraints associated with the traditional system were removed—and vastly more efficient means of mass mobilization through indoctrination and coercion became available—the restraints on power written into Leninist constitutions proved worthless.

Moreover, within the system itself, no meaningful checks and balances were created. The structure was pyramidal—the vital term, "democratic *centralism*." To be sure, the call was for the solicitation of the views of the people at the grassroots, via a network of local organizations. The formal defense of the "people's democratic socialist republic" was that the bottom initiated, the top disposed. But in its monopoly of power, the party vitiated any such idea, with its centralized power ultimately gravitating into the hands of one man. Herein lay the source of power for men like Stalin and Mao, and the crisis of succession in which their states were periodically involved. Even now, we see the system operating in its most pristine form in North Korea—officially the Democratic People's Republic of Korea.

To be sure, the real structure of authority was ever more complex as the Leninist societies evolved. I have always been uneasy with the totalitarian model because it signals a perfectibility that a society operated by humans cannot achieve and a staticism or permanence that is belied by current facts. As these societies evolved, a bureaucracy appropriate to Leninism in both its political and economic forms proliferated. In a paradoxical way, that bureaucracy was at once the champion of the status quo, hence, the supreme ruler, and the progressive usurper of his power. Men like Khrushchev and Mao railed against the bureaucratism that the system they staunchly espoused made inevitable. And while they could overreach the bureaucracy by fiat on occasion, they like others could never escape certain limits it imposed on them. It is in this sense that Weber and others are partially correct.

Even now, as we are witnessing a vast revolution throughout much of the Leninist world that will fundamentally alter that system, leadership has loomed up as of critical importance. One does not have to argue that the disappearance of Gorbachev would doom all Soviet reforms (a return to Stalinism, even Brezhnevism, is virtually impossible) to note the central role he is currently playing. Similarly, in China, Deng Xiaoping has been crucial as "paramount leader" at this point in modern China's troubled evolution.

Robert A. Scalapino

If authoritarian polities remain highly dependent on leaders, it would be a serious mistake to assume that democratic polities have become sufficiently institutionalized or that bureaucratic routinization in them has reached the point at which the role of leadership is of little consequence. Let us examine several cases. In the United States, no one fears that a president will break through institutional barriers to establish dictatorial power despite occasional legal transgressions. Yet, in recent years, leadership has been an important variable in shaping the political mood of the American people and their attachment to certain values and policies. A legitimate concern, moreover, is whether the quality and character of U.S. political leadership is being adversely affected by the merciless exposure given leaders and the ceaseless battle for control of public opinion that goes on between government and the media. The risk of a growing public cynicism or indifference is real, both in the United States and in other democratic societies. Are the penalties of political leadership in a modern democracy vastly overshadowing its rewards, except for a few individuals—not necessarily the best qualified?

Japan represents another interesting case.[1] It has often been said that modern Japan has not needed a dynamic leader, but—rather—an effective chairman of a corporative board. Historically, emotion could be channeled to the imperial institution, allowing governance to be in the hands of professional bureaucrats—in and out of the political parties.

Yet it is interesting to note that, at present, a crisis of leadership exists in Japan. At this writing, the prime minister, Toshiki Kaifu, is not accepted as a legitimate leader by many within his party, the political elite that has long governed the nation. The media also portray him as a transitional figure, holding office until the party elders can restore their reputations or select a "more suitable leader." Japan's postwar leaders have had legitimacy when they were able to coordinate party-bureaucratic governance, and through this, preside over economic and social policies satisfying a majority of the electorate. Now, however, both because of certain specific events such as the Recruit scandal and because of the rising power of new forces in Japanese politics, the required character of Japanese leadership is in flux. The restraints upon individual power are formidable—far more so than in the political cultures of the West—but the demands upon leaders, including the top leader, seem to be growing as further stages of Japanese democratization unfold with the trend toward inclusiveness, bringing the citizen more fully into the political process.

India provides yet another example of the crisis in democratic leadership. Rajiv Gandhi had to step down as India's prime minister, and the Congress party is in greater disarray than at any time in its recent history.[2] The political nature of the new nations that emerged after World War II was generally shaped by a nationalist movement, subsequently fashioned into a dominant party, with a leader emerging from its ranks. When the first revolutionary generation passes from the scene in such a setting, however, the democratic institutional structure is put to the test, assuming it has lasted through the initial period. Indian political institutions have now survived through several generations and, despite wide fissures within the society, hold the allegiance of a wide spectrum of political elites from the orthodox Hindus to the Communists. Yet Rajiv Gandhi epitomized the problem of the inheritance of power by an amateur. A similar problem exists in the Philippines, where Corazon Aquino had power thrust upon her despite her lack of preparation. The historic problem of monarchy was revisted on these societies: The necessary qualities of leadership cannot be transmitted genetically or through marriage.

If the politically open societies of today have great needs—and unique problems—relating to leadership, the uncertainties are especially clear in those societies that have recently moved from a status which I have labeled "authoritarian-pluralist," to experiment with democracy.[3] An authoritarian-pluralist society is one in which politics is characterized by limited if any competition and various restraints upon the political rights of the citizenry. Yet, in the social sphere, institutions like the church and educational organizations exist with some degree of independence from the state, and in the economic arena, the market plays the leading role, albeit with extensive state guidance in many cases.

Asia has had many authoritarian-pluralist states in this era, and some of them—for example, South Korea and Taiwan—have just entered a new political phase, marked by the advent of genuine choice for the citizen accompanied by a significant increase in political freedom. It remains to be seen how these experiments will evolve and what effect new institutions will have upon the nature of future leadership. Clearly, persuasion must supplant coercion as the primary source of effective governance, and legitimacy will hinge upon performance rather than faith. In these developments is summed up political modernization as the 20th century draws to a close.

In the light of these broad trends, let me briefly look at the problems of China's leadership during that nation's struggle to modernize. It is ironic that at the beginning of the 20th century a Chinese reform effort had just been crushed; certain officials were nonetheless calling for a turn outward to acquire science and technology, while at the same time demanding that Sinic political-cultural values be protected from pollution; yet official support was being given by the center to a xenophobic, anti-Western movement known abroad as the Boxer Rebellion; and the Old Buddha Cixi sat on the throne seeking to guide the nation amidst a deepening crisis, bewildered by a world she could not understand.[4] As this century draws to a close, the parallels with contemporary China are striking, although there are vitally important differences as well.

China remains a society in which the educated, articulate urban class is relatively small in numbers, dwarfed by the great peasant masses. To be sure, increasingly in the recent past, a portion of those masses have been climbing out of destitution and glimpsing what a better life could hold for them. Yet the traditional ways retain a powerful hold. In this setting and given China's heritage, leadership has continued to be cast in the mold of the father: stern, brooking no criticism, but—when responsible—prepared to listen to voices of those beneath him.

Paternalism is singular, not plural, and China has not known truly collective leadership, despite various forms of consultation and group inputs into the decision-making process. The principal oscillation, however, has been between a strong figure at the apex of the political-bureaucratic pyramid—symbolizing relative unity—and the absence of strength at the top—symbolizing the breakdown of order.

After the overthrow of the Manchu, Yuan Shikai made his bid for power, coming close to establishing a new dynasty. Nor was his the last such effort. Meanwhile, Sun Yat-sen's movement declined. In reorganizing his party in Tokyo in 1913, Sun demanded that its members obey him unswervingly so as to preserve unity. The commitment to strong leadership did not come only from the traditionalists.

While Sun's efforts during this period failed and China was plunged into the so-called "warlord" era, a new effort at centralization of authority via the Kuomintang soon got underway. As is well known, at the 1st KMT Congress in January 1924, the party—strongly influenced by the successful Bolshevik Revolution and with its representative in China, Michael Borodin, playing a significant role—adopted the Soviet organizational principles.[5] With some modifications, those principles have remained intact, despite vast changes in the political and economic climate.

It is not surprising, therefore, that under this system Chiang Kai-shek acquired very extensive personal power, and despite repeated attempts to challenge him—many of them involving violence—held that power through victory and defeat until his death. One can debate Chiang's strengths and weaknesses as a leader, but there can be no question that in his devotion to what he considered was good for China, and in his deep "Chineseness," namely, his commitment to certain traditional values and modes of behavior, he epitomized the dilemma of a transitional figure between the old politics and the new world.[6]

Meanwhile, Mao Zedong, another man caught between tradition and modernity, gradually fought and maneuvered his way to unchallengable power in the Communist party, and hence, after 1949, to the leadership of China. Mao combined a strong intellect with deeply rooted provincialism and a canny ability to fathom the strengths and weaknesses of others with an inability to form a lasting relationship with anyone—man or woman. His imprimatur still remains heavily stamped on his party and his state.

Deng Xiaoping is the Old Buddha who sits on China's throne today, having thrust himself and his country further into the modern era than those who preceded him. Yet he is still inhibited from going far beyond the past by many factors. Deng, less powerful than Mao at his zenith, must seek some consensus, although he appears to be the final authority. As he ponders priorities and reflects upon his and China's past, stability is given the greatest weight. The fear of chaos, the return of "warlordism"—or the Cultural Revolution—haunts the old men at the center and others as well, including many of the intellectuals out of sympathy with present government.

But how does one create stability—not just for the moment, but for the longer run—as a nation undergoes accelerating transformation? To this question, China's leaders have no suitable answer at present. The current efforts are to tighten surveillance while heightening indoctrination. Lei Feng, the idealized young soldier intended to be a model for China's youth, is back. Mao is again being elevated. And Deng's collected works are being assigned. Everyone is attending more political education programs to cleanse his mind of polluting thoughts.

In its extreme form, this is stability of the Kim Il-sung or Ceaucescu type, and it has no long-term future. In present-day China, it is likely to produce more cynics than true believers. In a dynamic, changing society, genuine stability paradoxically can be maintained only when the system permits questioning, dissent, and political choice before discontent reaches an explosive level.

It was the recognition of this fact in the last years of his life that distinguished Chiang Ching-kuo both from his father and from other elders of modern China. As one reflects upon young Chiang's life, the panorama of modern China comes into focus. Born into a traditional setting, offspring of an arranged marriage, Ching-kuo grew up in what we would term today a broken home. His father must have been a somewhat distant and aloof if strongly paternalistic figure. From Chiang Kai-shek's diary, we can glimpse the father-son relationship. In letters sent to Ching-kuo, there were repeated exhortations to take care of his younger brother, to study hard, and observe the classical rules of Chinese decorum. Occasionally, the father would correct Ching-kuo's misdrawn characters via a letter to the boy, serving as auxiliary teacher. But in the youth's formative years, the relationship was generally marked by irregular contacts.[7] A father increasingly preoccupied with matters beyond the family and a man having little in common with his wife were hardly rarities in China—then and now. The wonder is how, under conditions of lengthy separation, the family bond—at least in certain of its dimensions—remains as strong as it does.

When Chiang Ching-kuo was still a boy, only 15 years of age, he was sent to the Soviet Union, traveling aboard a ship that departed from Shanghai in October 1925.[8] This extraordinary adventure was no accident. At this point, the 1st Kuomintang-Communist alliance was in effect, and an agreement to send Chinese students to the newly established Sun Yat-sen University in Moscow had been concluded. Ching-kuo's father, moreover, was currently commandant at the Whampoa Military Academy, the Kuomintang's premier military-political training center. He was also accounted as a member of the party's "Left wing" as well as playing the leading military role in these years. Chiang's son should have had a special status with Soviet as well as Chinese revolutionary authorities.

Young Chiang's first political commitments thus came naturally, a product of his environment and the times. In China, just prior to his departure for the Soviet Union, he had been caught up in the nationalist fervor that swept over Chinese urban students after the May 30th Incident of 1925. He had joined the Kuomintang. Very shortly after his schooling in Moscow began, he became a member of the Communist Youth League, and later affiliated with the Trotsky faction. In his brief memoirs on his years in the U.S.S.R., he makes it clear that in this course he was influenced by several of his teachers as well as Karl Radek, head of the university and a leading Trotsky adherent.

When his father turned against the Communists in Shanghai in April 1927, and ordered their suppression, Ching-kuo bitterly condemned him, writing highly critical articles. Yet the unfolding Stalin-Trotsky struggle caught the young Chinese sojourner in hits web as it did many other Chinese students. A majority of the Chinese Communist party leaders maintained their loyalty to Stalin and, from an overseas office in Moscow, sought to keep a close surveillance over the Chinese students studying in the U.S.S.R. According to Ching-kuo, it was they who determined that he should remain in Russia rather than go home after his graduation from Sun Yat-sen University in April 1927.

The saga of Chiang Ching-kuo's life for the next decade need not be repeated here in detail. From his own account, he continued his commitment to the Communist cause in the early years that followed, joining the Red Army as an enlisted man and after one year being selected as a trainee in the Central Military and Political Institute located in Leningrad. In the course of his training, he separated himself from the Trotsky faction and became a candidate member of the Russian Communist party. Yet, according to his record, the CCP branch in Moscow continued to hound him repeatedly in the years that followed, interfering with his career opportunities and forcing him out of Moscow, with much of the subsequent years spent in the Urals and Siberia. Ching-kuo's opportunity to return to China came in the spring of 1937, in the aftermath of the Sian Incident involving his father's detention and the subsequent onset of the 2nd Kuomintang-Communist detente.

Chiang Ching-kuo had departed from China as a callow teenager lacking in the most elementary political or social preparation for the events that lay ahead. He returned 12 years later, veteran of various political battles, having experienced a series of highs and lows in his personal life and well acquainted with the seamy side of Soviet society as well as the finality of decisions made by those wielding supreme power in such a state.

It would be difficult not to believe that, in these years, young Chiang acquired a toughness—product of hardship and repeated failure—that was to stay with him in the future. If his brief memoirs can be taken as a guide, moreover, his real bitterness was directed not at the Russians, not even the high officials with whom he came into contact, but at those senior cadres who represented the Chinese Communist party in the Soviet capital. And despite his long stay in the U.S.S.R. and his marriage to a Russian, Chiang Ching-kuo was not Russianized. He returned to China a Chinese.

Whether it was easy or difficult for Ching-kuo to reestablish a relationship with his father is not clear. It would appear, however, that Chiang Kai-shek eventually came to trust his elder son as he trusted few others. Ching-kuo's first important assignment was to serve as commissioner of South Kiangsi—the very region in which

Chu Teh and Mao had established their initial guerrilla base. Soon it was to be largely isolated as the Japanese secured coastal China. At the close of the war, Chiang Ching-kuo was first given the assignment of negotiating with the Russians a treaty in the aftermath of the Yalta agreements, and subsequently, he was to serve in Manchuria, then in Shanghai, as deputy supervisor of the Economic Control Council. The latter assignment came during the darkest days of the Nationalist government, with the military front collapsing and inflation raging out of control. Ching-kuo acquired a reputation for ruthlessness during this period, but no amount of toughness could compensate for the disintegration of political and social order that had accompanied the war in China and the colossal errors of the Kuomintang in its initial postwar policies.

Few leaders have been subjected to such an unending succession of failures as Chiang Ching-kuo. From his youth to his early middle age, he had been on the losing side, with rare moments of triumph such as the allied victory over Japan in mid-1945. Nor was the specter of defeat quickly removed after the Nationalist retreat to Taiwan. The Nationalist occupation of that island was deeply resented by a significant number of the Chinese who considered themselves natives of Taiwan and who had lived for half a century under Japanese rule. The bitterness, moreover, was greatly enhanced by the bloody Nationalist suppression of the 1947 uprising, with thousands of casualties. In the opening years of the Nationalist era on Taiwan, moreover, the victorious Communists loomed up as an ever-present threat. Perhaps the Kuomintang should thank Kim Il-sung for drawing the Chinese Communists into another conflict and, at the same time, causing the United States to reexamine its earlier abandonment of the KMT. Just as Mao owed a heavy debt to the Japanese for his ultimate victory in a war-torn China, Chiang Kai-shek survived at least in part because of the Korean War.

The years after 1949, however, were rugged ones for the Kuomintang, and Chiang Ching-kuo's reputation was not enhanced by the fact that he was placed in charge of internal security and intelligence. The severity of his policies during the final period in Shanghai was carried over to Taiwan at a time when the risks—internal and external—seemed extraordinarily high. During this period, he surrounded himself with men who combined unquestioned loyalty with an essential simplicity relating to politics and focusing upon a deep hatred of communism. They served him well, but because the end justified any means, they also created an atmosphere of justified fear in many quarters.

It was not until the death of his father in 1975 that Chiang Ching-kuo came fully into his own, although he held the premiership from 1972. Through the previous years he had been the filial son, possessed of his father's trust and hence given great authority, but properly deferential both in public and in private. At this point, Ching-kuo was no longer young and one would have presumed that both his political views and his methods of governance would have been fixed. Yet the basic task confronting him had changed. The primary need no longer revolved around security. Nor did it lie in the initiation of a new economic program: the Taiwan economy had already begun its rapid acceleration. The critical need now was to promote the movement of the society over which he had control in such a fashion that politics would begin to catch up to the social and economic realities of a dramatically new era.

In this, he succeeded. Thus, the most fitting epitaph for Chiang Ching-kuo's career would be a simple yet profoundly important one: "He could evolve in accordance with the necessities of his times." It is precisely in this respect that the ultimate quality of his leadership was revealed. At earlier points, to be sure, he had exhibited the traits of the benevolent ruler, taking field trips to see conditions for himself, and mingling with the common people. But, in the final years of his life, recognizing that the time had come for a widening of the political process—a new type of political inclusiveness—he progressively removed restrictions on civil liberties and permitted the existence of a more open society. In the initial stages, the political changes were de facto more than de jure, but they were increasingly recognized as changes by the citizenry nevertheless. To be sure, there were transgressions of the old type, some of them serious, but the broad trend toward greater political openness went forward.

No one has argued that the transformation of an authoritarian state into a democracy is an easy process, especially when the political traditions of the society are largely in opposition to democratic values and procedures. Not infrequently, setbacks ensue, and failure cannot be ruled out. Yet Taiwan continues on a path today that was charted by Chiang Ching-kuo and some of the progressive minded men whom he supported in the final period of his life. Of course there were pressures of many sorts—both internal and external—that operated on behalf of such change. When has a leader not been subject to and affected by such pressures? Yet there were alternative paths Ching-kuo might have chosen, one being a renewal of tighter security measures in an effort to distinguish dissidents. While that route would have inevitably failed, it would have produced a tragic era for the entire society. Thus, even if the path was zigzag at times, it went in the proper general direction. In sum, in choosing the appropriate priority, in selecting individuals capable of concentrating on that priority, in broadening the government's appeals to Taiwan's citizenry, and in timing the changes sufficiently well to make a reasonable degree of success possible, Chiang Ching-kuo fulfilled the requirements of the effective leader.

Let me conclude with a few thoughts about political leadership in the tempestuous times that lie ahead. First, the need can only increase for leaders that can articulate the problems of modern society for the average citizen and provide that citizen with an action program suited to the resolution or amelioration of those problems. It is the task of the intellectual to live with complexity. It is the task of the political leader to make that complexity understandable to the citizen without unduly distorting it. And that is not easy at a time when people everywhere are being assaulted by an unprecedented volume of "information," often deeply contradictory in both its presentation of "fact" and interpretation. Yet, however strong the institutions of governance, however powerful the faceless officials who attend to the technical tasks, citizens will continue to demand a certain personalization of their political system in the form of an individual who can symbolize their values and who can persuade them of the need for a given course of action.

Second, while the need for leadership remains great, it is legitimate to worry about the quality of leadership in this age, as noted earlier. Militant pressure groups are emerging, some of them single-issue in nature. Not infrequently, they are committed to tactics outside the perimeters of the democratic system, and often they seek to coerce leaders through a variety of threats. It is grueling to be harassed by those for whom compromise—the essence of open politics—is a dirty word. In the age of "scientific public opinion polls," moreover, a broader problem lurks. To what extent should a leader lead, and to what extent should he or she follow? Unless one has extraordinary powers of persuasion, the risks of pursuing one's conscience instead of following the majority (even if it is wrong) have greatly increased.

As is well known, we have also stripped leaders of virtually all privacy in advanced democratic societies. Investigatory journalism is in its heyday. Perhaps the citizenry has the right to know the personal peccadillos of leaders, but there are few perfect individuals. Who among past American leaders could have survived in the current climate—Lincoln (who, it is now reported, padded his expense account), Roosevelt, or Kennedy (both of whom had extramarital affairs, the latter in abundance)? How far does the right to know extend? And should it extent to personalities of the media who are now major forces in the political arena through their selection and interpretation of the news?

In any case, the force of ideology will continue to decline in virtually all societies. Leaders in many societies will find it frustrating to deal in pragmatic, problem-oriented fashion with a myriad of problems without being able to bind the citizens to an indissoluble unity by some powerful ideology. Yet, despite a few upsurges, blind faith is being replaced in the overwhelming majority of states by the test of performance. That means that most leaders will have to be satisfied with 60 percent or even 51 percent voter support. Indeed, some will have to live with less approval, holding on either through coercion or because election time has not come.

Finally, leaders adjudged by history as "great" will in no small part be made by the times and the opportunities given them. There are certain periods when no one has the possibility of success. Those ill-fated to serve in such times can only lament their fortune. But the essence of "greatness" in any case lies in the capacity to discern the fundamental nature of one's time—and more than discern, to anticipate that nature, then shape values and policies that accord with it. Thus, whatever the difficulties, there is ample opportunity for "greatness" in the decades immediately ahead.

Robert A. Scalapino

ENDNOTES

1. Recent general studies of Japanese politics of worth are Gerald L. Curtis, *The Japanese Way of Politics*, Columbia University Press, New York, 1988, and Takeshi Ishida and Ellis S. Krauss, eds., *Democracy in Japan*, University of Pittsburgh Press, Pittsburgh, 1989.

2. Late developments in Indian politics are well sketched by Richard Sisson, "India in 1989—A Year of Elections in a Culture of Change," *Asian Survey*, February 1990, pp. 111-125.

3. See this author's *The Politics of Development—Perspectives on Twentieth-Century Asia*, Harvard University Press, Cambridge, Massachusetts, 1989.

4. An interpretive study of this era is contained in a book by this author and George T. Yu, *Modern China and Its Revolutionary Process—Recurrent Challenges to the Traditional Order, 1850-1920*, University of California Press, Berkeley, 1985. See especially Chapter 2, pp. 38-108.

5. The Kuomintang Archives in Taipei contain an extensive transcript of the 1st Congress used by this author and George Yu in preparation for the second volume of the above work. On Borodin's role in China, see Lydia Holubnychy, *Michael Borodin and the Chinese Revolution, 1923-1925*, East Asian Institute, Columbia University, New York, 1979.

6. Among the many studies of Chiang Kai-shek, one of the most stimulating has unfortunately not been published. It is the work by Pinchon Y. Y. Loh, *The Political Vision of Chiang Kai-shek: Public Symbols and Private Meanings*, as well as his earlier work, *The Early Chiang Kai-shek: A Study of his Personality and Politics*, Columbia University Press, New York, 1971. For a

voluminous work sympathetic to Chiang with a wealth of data gleaned from his private papers, see Keiji Furuya, *Chiang Kai-Shek—His Life and Times* (English edition by Chun-Ming Chang, St. John's University, New York, 1981). See also Ch'in Hsiao-i, *Chiang tsung-t'ung ta-shih ch'ang-pien* (A Chronological Account of Important Events Concerning President Chiang), 6 Vols., Taipei, 1967. Another vitally important document is *Chiang ts'an-mou-chang, jih-chi* (Diary of Chief-of-Staff Chiang), in the Kuomintang Historical Archives.

7. Ibid.

8. A brief account of Chiang Ching-kuo's years in the Soviet Union is contained as an appendix in Ray S. Cline, *Chiang Ching-kuo Remembered—The Man and His Political Legacy*, United States Global Strategy Council, Washington, D.C., 1989. It was written by Chiang in May 1937, shortly after his return from the U.S.S.R. and is entitled in English, "My Days in Soviet Russia," pp. 147-187.

Editor and Contributor Information

RALPH CLOUGH is Adjunct Professor of International Affairs at the Johns Hopkins University. Among his publications are *Island China* and *East Asia and U.S. Security*.

JOHN FEI is Professor of Economics at Yale University. His books include *Growth with Equity: The Taiwan Case* and *Transition of Open Dualist Economy*.

HELENA V. S. HO is a Researcher in Asian Studies at Columbia University.

BRIAN HOOK, former Editor of *The Chinese Quarterly*, is Professor of Chinese Studies at the University of Leeds. He is also the editor of *The Cambridge Encyclopedia of China*.

CHO-YUN HSU is University Professor of History at the University of Pittsburgh. *Ancient China in Transition* and *Han Agriculture* are among his books.

SHAO-CHUAN LENG is Compton Professor of Government and Chairman of the Committee on Asian Studies at the University of Virginia. Among his publications relating to the Republic of China are *Sun Yat-sen and Communism* and *Coping with Crises: How Governments Deal with Emergencies*.

THOMAS METZGER is Senior Fellow of the Hoover Institution at Stanford University. His publications include *The Internal Organization of Ch'ing Bureaucracy* and *Escape from*

Predicament: Neo-Confucianism and China's Evolving Political Culture.

ANDREW NATHAN is Professor of Political Science at Columbia University. His books include *Chinese Democracy* and *China's Crisis: Dilemmas of Reform and Prospects for Democracy.*

ROBERT SCALAPINO is Robson Professor of Government Emeritus at the University of California at Berkeley. His recent publications include *Modern China and its Revolutionary Process* and *The Politics of Development: Perspectives on Twentieth-Century Asia.*

EDWIN WINCKLER is Professor of the East Asian Institute at Columbia University. His latest publication is *Contending Approaches to the Political Economy of Taiwan.*

Index

Brzezinski, Zbigniew, 137

Carter, Jimmy, 41, 137, 146, 148, 149

Ch'en Ch'eng, 10, 112

Ch'en Wen-ch'eng, 45, 47, 167

Chang Chün-hung, 40

Chao Shao-k'ang, 46

Chiang Ching-kuo, chronology of life, 24-27; death of mother, 7; as defense minister and premier, 13-15; early life, 1-3, 200-201; early years on Taiwan, 10-13, 50; and ROC economy, 63-88, 89-101; education of, 2, 3-4, 6-7, 18; foreign assessments of, 163-186; and foreign policy, 133-159; and internal security and intelligence, 11-12, 42-43, 50, 113; and Japan, 7; in Kiangsi, 5-7; leadership of, 199-206; marriage to Fang Liang, 4, 165, 175, 178, 180, 201; and May 30th incident, 2; and opposition parties, 17, 40, 42, 171; and People's Republic of China, 115-121, 133, 152-157; postwar years, 8-9; and reform, 31-55, 151-152, 183-185; relationship with Chiang Kai-shek, 2-5, 198-199; and social policy, 103-121; and U.S.S.R., 3-4, 11, 178, 180-181; and United States, 133

Chiang Hsiao-wu, 48, 172

Chiang Hsiao-yung, 48

INDEX

Chiang Kai-shek, 2-5, 7, 9, 10, 12, 51, 111, 134, 136, 140-142, 175, 181, 198-199; relationship with Chiang Ching-kuo, 2-5, 198-199

Chiang Wei-kuo, 48, 172

Chiang Yen-Shih, 45

China, People's Republic of (PRC), official reaction to death of Chiang Ching-kuo, 164-166; relations with Republic of China, 15, 36-38, 139-143, 152-157; relations with United States, 14, 15, 36, 147, 150, 169

China, Republic of (ROC), early years under KMT, 10-11; economic statistics, 20-23, 168; economy of, 14-16, 63-86, 89-101, 139, 144, 156, 158; relations with People's Republic of China, 15, 36-38, 139-143, 152-157; relations with United States, 133, 135-139, 145-152, 169; and United Nations, 143

Christopher, Warren, 148

Chow Shu-kai, 136

Chu Fu-Sung, 147

Chu Teh, 202

Chu-yu Chao, 13

Communist International, 3

Communist party of China, 10, 39, 164-165, 169-170

Democratic Progress party (DPP), 16, 44, 174, 177, 185

Deng Xiaoping, 38, 141, 153, 157, 170, 172, 194, 198-199

"Four Dragons" (Taiwan, Singapore, Hong Kong, and South Korea), 67, 69, 75-76

INDEX

Fu Tso-yi, 140

Hong Kong, 67, 69, 75-76; and reaction to death of Chiang Ching-Kuo, 166-176

Hsu Hsin-liang, 40

Hua Guofeng, 141-142

Huang Hsin-chieh, 40

Huang Zhen, 137

Japan, 4, 5, 7, 8, 14, 195; and ROC, diplomatic relations with, 144-145; and ROC economy, 65, 67, 69, 74, 94; and occupation of Taiwan, 10; reaction to death of Chiang Ching-kuo, 174-176

Joint Commission of Rural Reconstruction (JCRR), 10, 12, 113, 117

K'ang Yu'wei, 93

Kang Ning-hsiang, 40, 46, 174

Kennedy, Edward, 36

Kim Il-sung, 193, 202

Kissinger, Henry, 136

Kuomintang (KMT), 3, 10-11, 200; ideology of, 90, 103-110; and opposition, 41, 151; and reform, 32-55, 183-185; and social policy, 115-120; structure of state under, 3, 113-115

Kuznets, Simon, 66-67, 74

Leach, Jim, 36

Lee Teng-hui, 47, 159, 172, 175-177, 179-180, 182

INDEX

Li Huan, 49

Li, K. T., 85

Li Ta-chao, 3

Liang Ch'i-ch'ao, 93

Lin Yi-hsiung, 45

Liu, Henry, 36, 45, 47, 167

Ma Chi-chuang, 155

Ma Ying-jeou, 36, 39, 46, 49

Mao Zedong, 7, 8, 194, 198, 202

Mathis, Dawson, 137

May Fourth Movement, 4

Nixon, Richard, 135-136

Opium War, 64

Pell, Claiborne, 36

Philippines, 91, 196

Qu Wu, 165

Reagan, Ronald, 37, 149

Rogers, William, 136

Shen Chang-huan, 134, 145, 147, 155

INDEX

Shen, James, 136

Solarz, Stephen, 36

Stalin, Joseph, 4, 9, 180-181, 200

Stepan, Alfred, 32, 53

Su Nan-ch'eng, 40

Sun Yat-sen, 2, 8, 16, 51, 70, 90, 93, 99-100, 108, 111, 184, 198

Sun Yun-suan, 13, 47, 112, 119, 155

T'ao Pai-ch'uan, 42

Tao, S. T., 13

"Ten Major Construction Projects," 14, 63, 64-65, 78

"Three Principles of the People," 7, 39, 51

Tsiang, Y. S., 12, 13, 155

Union of Soviet Socialist Republics (Russia), 2, 3, 11; official reaction to death of Chiang Ching-kuo, 179

United States, relations with People's Republic of China, 14, 15, 36, 147, 150, 169; relations with Republic of China (Taiwan), 133, 135-139, 145-152, 169; and Taiwan Relations Act, 148, 169

Unger, Leonard, 137, 138, 147

Vance, Cyrus, 137, 145

Wang, Chia-hua, 35-36

Wang Sheng, 47, 155

INDEX

Wu Kuo-chen, 178

Wu San-lien, 42

Wu Xiuquan, 142

Yang, H. K., 148

Yao Chia-wen, 40

Yen Chia-kan, 134

Yen Fu, 93

Yen Jianying, 152

Yu Kuo-hua, 112, 119, 175

Yuan, Shikai, 198

Zhao Ziyang, 164, 170

Zhou Enlai, 140-141, 178

Zhou, Nan, 165

HARVARD-YENCHING LIBRARY

This book must be returned to the Library on or before the last date stamped below. A fine will be charged for late return. Non-receipt of overdue notices does not exempt the borrower from fines.

DEC 17 1996
MAY 1 1997
MAY 28 2000
MAY 29 2001
JUN 2 2007
MAY 2002
FEB 2003
FEB 10 2005